THIS BOOK BELONGS TO

_____

RECIPES FROM A VERY SMALL ISLAND

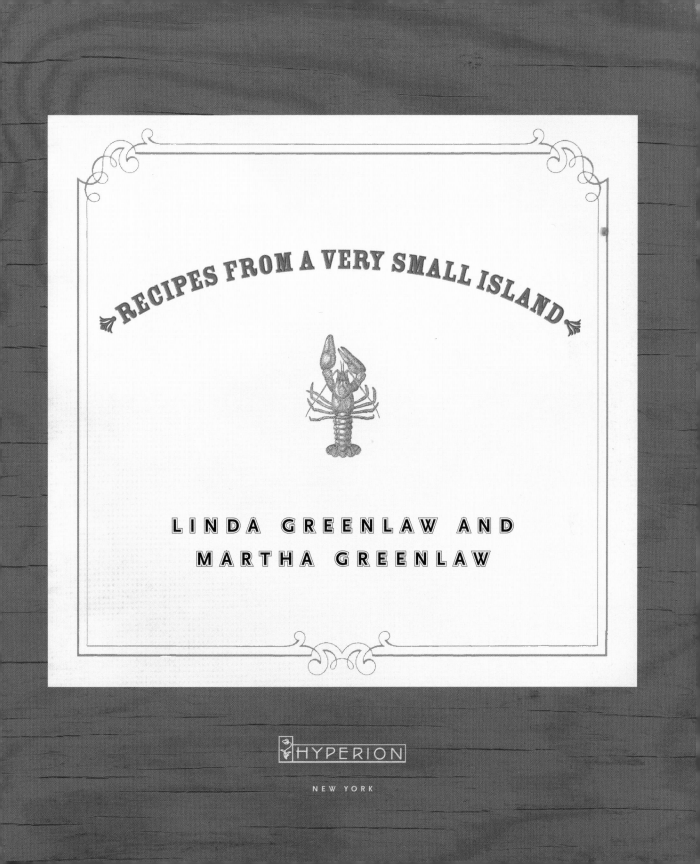

LINDA GREENLAW AND MARTHA GREENLAW

HYPERION

NEW YORK

ISBN 1-4013-0073-1

Book Design by

JOOYOUNG LEE
HSU + ASSOCIATES

Hyperion books are available for special promotions and premiums.
For details contact Michael Rentas, Assistant Director, Inventory Operations,
Hyperion, 77 West 66th Street, 11th floor,
New York, New York 10023, or call 212-456-0133.

First Edition
10   9   8   7   6   5   4   3   2   1

DEDICATION

This book is dedicated to Jim, my husband, Linda's Dad, and our best friend.

Thanks, Jim, for your patience, sense of humor, and being there for me through the

hard times as well as the good times, during sickness and health.

— Martha

RECIPES FROM A VERY SMALL ISLAND

CONTENTS

LINDA'S PREFACE

MY MOTHER, MARTHA LOUISE GREENLAW, will not become the next Martha Stewart. She has never made her own Christmas ornaments, nor has she ever recycled the cardboard tube at the center of the toilet paper roll in the cause of home decorating. "Our" Martha does not knit, crochet, or sew, which is why I learned to hem pant legs with a stapler. I clearly recall an old cookie tin referred to as "the sewing basket" which I discovered under Mom's bed while searching for something with which to replace a renegade button, and my dismay at its contents of abundant iron-on patches and safety pins and its lack of needles and thread. Housekeeping was somewhat of a fire drill, done only when certain company was expected, and then at the last minute. Working as a team, Mom and four children could tidy the twelve disheveled rooms at Seventeen White Street in sixty minutes flat. I do not remember what was stored in my bedroom's bureau drawers, but it was not clothing. Laundry for six family members could be found in one of two places: Dirty duds were in a heap on the basement floor under the laundry chute that pierced three stories, and clean clothes lived in piles that lined the stairway leading to the bedrooms. Mom cheerfully endured some lighthearted teasing from her father-in-law about her unique form of domesticity, but the teasing stopped at dinnertime.

A seat at the table at my mother's house is a privilege I, at the age of forty-four, still look forward to today. The sanctity of mealtime is bolstered by strict rules set by our unwavering Martha. Shirts and shoes are required and hats are forbidden. The television and stereo are shut off prior to our sitting down. Electronic games and cell phones are neither seen nor heard. There will be some semblance of manners, although speaking with one's mouth full is permitted when complimenting the chef. All of this may sound daunting to the "eat on the run" crowd, but the mealtime regimen is as comforting as the food itself. Food in abundance is a sign of well-being and prosperity for a generation that knows what it feels like to be rationed or even to go to bed hungry. I have never been truly hungry, but I understand the feeling of refuge when being fed. My mother makes

every meal a communal event whether it's a feast for a cast of thousands or the occasional sandwich just for the two of us. Laughter and singing come from my mother's kitchen and follow her from the stove to the table, where every morsel is a celebration.

Just over five feet tall and weighing well under 120 pounds, Mom at the age of seventy-one is still a giant in the kitchen. There's an aura about Mom when she's cooking and entertaining that extends to and envelops all who are included: a beam of sunshine absent the glare, which warms recipients of this gift of food that she enthusiastically and generously shares. For food is her gift and her passion. I have occasionally helped Mom in the kitchen from as far back as I can remember, and although I have developed my own culinary sense and flair, she reigns. Whether we are working in her kitchen, my kitchen, or somewhere in between, she possesses an absolute, unspoken, and natural authority. No formal training, no degrees from prestigious institutions, neither gourmet nor chef, but Martha Greenlaw is a cook. And where we come from, no higher compliment can be paid. *lg*

MARTHA'S INTRODUCTION

WE NEW ENGLANDERS ARE A STURDY BREED and tend to stay pretty much where we're born. Nowhere is this more true than in Maine. I am well aware of the hardships of living along Maine's rocky coast and of the even more strenuous ones of living further inland, but I am also aware of the privilege. Maine is my home, Maine is where my heart is. It's breathtakingly beautiful, still not crowded, and, like the rest of New England, attracts feisty, independent people. This is just fine by me!

I have been cooking New England food for too many years to mention, and along the way I have developed a reputation for being a pretty good cook. I love time in the kitchen, and when you can start with some of the best native ingredients around, cooking is more of a pleasure than ever.

Cooking up here in the north country is as much driven by ingredients as by creativity. When I see a basket of tiny Maine blueberries, I know it's time to make a blueberry pie. When my husband, Jim, brings a few lobsters home after a day on the lobster boat, the *Mattie Belle*, I boil them right up. When I spot fresh green beans in the local store, I buy them and cook them that night. Nothing fancy, but always good.

Why I Wrote This Book

I HAVE FOUR CHILDREN, ALL LIVING HERE IN MAINE. My second daughter, Linda, is an author, as well as a lobster fisherman and a very good cook. She used to be a swordfish boat captain, sailing out of Massachusetts all the way to the Grand Banks, but a few years ago she returned to our little island community and took up lobstering with her dad. She has written three books about these experiences and so I guess it was natural for us to start talking about writing a cookbook together. Both of us have strong opinions about food and cooking and both of us love to eat.

Linda and I are passionate about the fish, lobster, and crabs in our Maine waters and the blueberries and cranberries that grow so easily along our coast. We also love all manner of meat and fowl. Both of us have been known to plan entire parties around a single ingredient and so, when we sat down to organize this book into chapters, we decided it should be done as much as possible by ingredient.

As you flip through the pages, you'll find the lobster, crab, clam, mussel, shrimp, and scallop recipes together in one chapter and all the fin fish together in another. We put the blueberry and cranberry recipes together, mixing savory and sweet preparations. We combined the meat and poultry dishes in one chapter, too.

If you've ever tried to organize your own recipe files, you will understand that even these neat and tidy categories have blurry edges. For instance, we have a chapter called Beginnings, which has recipes that involve crab, clams, or shrimp. In Chapter 9, Plain Old-Fashioned Sweets, you won't find sweet blueberry or cranberry dishes.

People who visit New England during the spectacular months of July and August dream about our lobster rolls, clam chowder, coleslaw, and blueberry pancakes. These are pretty much "summer foods," and as outstanding as they are—and we have recipes for all of them in the book—there's more to New England cooking. We are known, too, for our baked beans, Boston brown bread, pumpkin pie, and gingerbread, foods that taste awfully good during cold New England winters.

I count myself lucky to have cooked with wonderful friends and family members over the years and so have included recipes from many of them, too. We are no more stuck in the past in New England than elsewhere, and we like to experiment with the flavors and simplified cooking techniques that constitute contemporary American cooking. You'll find recipes for salmon with a blueberry salsa, a tricolor beet salad, and even lobster chili! (Try it; I was wary, too, until I tasted it.)

Linda has supplied about twenty recipes for the book, which I love. I think she's an adventuresome cook, with good ideas and no hesitation about trying them. She's supplied the essays about the food and island life, something she is far better equipped to do than I.

I am always on the lookout for new and intriguing recipes and have never been afraid to try unfamiliar foods. One year when the kids were young, I took an intensive course in Chinese cooking. I remember how much I loved the challenge, even if Linny and my other kids refer to that period as "the year of Chinese cooking."

Isle au Haut

OUR TINY ISLAND OFF THE TIP OF STONINGTON, Maine, is home to Jim and me. Linny has settled here, too, and while all of us spend time "off island" and enjoy being out in the larger world, our return to the island is always on our minds. Jim's mother and grandparents were born here, members of the Hamilton and Robinson families, who, for generations, have lived on the island and elsewhere in our part of Penobscot Bay. I was known as a highlander when I was younger, having been born on a dairy farm in Winslow, Maine, which was at least a good hour from the coast. I didn't set foot on the island until 1957, when Jim brought me here on a most memorable date, and there was no turning back after my first taste of it.

We had to stop first in Rockland to pick up Jim's grandmother, Lil, who accompanied us to Isle au Haut as our chaperone. It was a glorious fall weekend in Maine and as we walked the short route from the dock to the old Greenlaw homestead, I felt myself falling in love with the place. We had a simple supper that night in a house lit mainly by kerosene lamps. I remember Lil's biscuits, which were similar to my mother's. The next morning we ate a big breakfast of eggs, bacon, and potatoes, and I was enchanted with how the autumn sunshine sparkled on the ocean. I just knew I was home.

A year later, Jim and I were married and although we lived in Topsham, Maine, we came to the island as often as possible and certainly most of every summer. Finally, after our children were raised, we moved here as full-time residents and I couldn't be happier.

Because there is a permanent population of about forty-five people and a summer one of only four hundred or so, everyone knows their neighbors and there is a lot of casual socializing. Island life may be relaxed, but it is not always easy.

Linda and I agree you have to be independent, resourceful, and tough to live out here. The rewards are many: a sense of tranquility and peace that comes with the slower pace and natural beauty. But I would argue that best of all is the sense of community, and for me, that community is always enhanced by good food.

Over the years, we've had more potluck suppers and family picnics on the island than you can count. Off island, when we lived nearer Portland, Maine, Jim and I were active in a gourmet group and got together monthly for what we dubbed "the galloping indigestion" dinners. Truth be told, the food was awfully good and many of the recipes I perfected then are included here. For instance, I have been making the Make-Ahead Party Potatoes on page 187 for years, and they are still a big hit.

When the children were young, they played for hours with their cousins and friends, running from house to house on the island. We prepared a lot of communal meals then, moving in and out of each other's kitchens with familiarity. Every night after supper, the kids gathered at the Kennedy

Field to play softball, capture the flag, or hide 'n' seek. We are so far north, it doesn't get dark until late in the summer, so these games could go on for hours. The field, which is in front of the Congregational Church, is the largest piece of open land on the island.

Sometimes there was a dance at the town hall, which still doubles as a library and a gym. After these dances, Linny tells me she and her teenage friends would walk around the island. We have only one road, but it's thirteen miles long! That was quite a hike for the kids, but since there are hardly any cars on the road at any time of day and since there was no place to go, we never worried.

The island hasn't changed much. We have a one-room schoolhouse and a post office the size of a playhouse. There's still only one store, open in the summer from 9 to 5 and in the winter from 10 to 1, with a limited selection. Most of us leave the island once a week and haul groceries and other supplies home on the mail boat that serves as our ferry. You might think we would have extensive vegetable and herb gardens, but unless you erect a very high deer fence, it's not realistic.

Generally, islanders have an old car on the island and then another, somewhat better car, in Stonington to use when we leave. Island kids have been known to take our cars for joyrides from time to time; so, to avoid having them broken into, most of us just leave the keys in the cars when we park them at the dock.

Although we have to ship all supplies to the island and therefore have to come up with ingenious ways to store things, we have all the luxuries of mainland living, even if they are a little more haphazard. For example, the electricity is quite reliable and only goes out during the worst storms, but the electric bills are another matter. The Isle au Haut electric company is located in someone's house, and the company owner (who is also the homeowner) sends the bills when he gets around to it—which is never on schedule!

I wouldn't trade any of this for another way of life. When I was young, I couldn't wait to get off the farm where I grew up, one of six children—although today I would give anything to go back there just to smell the aroma of new mown hay coming through my bedroom window. My mother was an excellent cook and while she didn't encourage our help in the kitchen, later when I had my own family and started cooking all the time, I realized I was competing with her. I thank her for the inspiration.

Cooking on the Island

AS I HAVE SAID, LINDA AND I are opinionated about our food. We are of the opinion that it has to taste good and that it should be shared with family and friends. This is why we wrote the book: to share our cooking with you.

This is not a lobster cookbook, although we could write one. For good reason, Maine lobsters are legendary and while we, as a lobstering family, sometimes get tired of them, we wouldn't want to go for too long without eating lobster. Linda likes to boil them outside to keep them from steaming up the house; I don't mind cooking them inside. She has a deep pot on her deck, originally designed for deep-frying turkey, that she fires up at any time and can hold up to eighteen lobsters.

We both prefer soft-shell lobsters (more about these in Chapter 2) and we like to cook them in plain, unsalted water. Why cook the lobsters in seawater? They are salty enough. We don't like to bake them topped with seaweed, either, which tends to discolor the meat. In other words, when it comes to lobster, we're purists. But we also have been known to participate in a clambake, a traditional New England beach picnic that includes lobsters under seaweed, steamed clams, as well as other dishes. We like to take along clam chowder, coleslaw, and a blueberry pie to round out the meal, recipes which are included in the book. I love Linda's true feelings about putting on a clambake, which she wrote about on page 45!

We feel equally passionate about cranberries and blueberries. We have small, natural cranberry bogs on the island that don't produce enough cranberries for much more than cranberry sauce at Thanksgiving—and then only if you get there before the birds do—but it's fun to search for the red berries in the late fall. Luckily, there are wonderful cranberries from downstate and nearby Massachusetts that we happily consume.

The birds like our blueberries, too. These tiny treasures are more plentiful than cranberries on the island and it's a common summertime activity to pick them from the wild bushes that grow just about anywhere. If you've never eaten a Maine blueberry, you are in for a treat. They are smaller and more intense than the common, cultivated ones.

As I have said, there is more to New England cooking than lobster and cranberries, and a lot of it is here, seen through the prism of my experiences, prejudices, and enthusiasms. For example, you can cook a traditional New England–style Thanksgiving dinner from this book, make a Fourth of July picnic, throw a dinner party, or prepare a simple lunch for your kids. And why not? I've been doing it for years!

No island is an island. Even though we are a tiny community seven miles off the coast, we relish being part of Maine, and New England—and draw huge pleasure from our friends and family who live throughout the state and the region. In this book, we hope to introduce you to our island, our friends, our family, and of course, our food. *mg*

CHAPTER 1

BEGINNINGS

DICK'S AMAZING STUFFED CLAMS

ONE OF OUR FAVORITE ISLAND SUMMER ACTIVITIES is clam digging. We gather our clam

hoes and clam roller (basket), drive over to the east side of the island, and walk out to the flats at Old Rich's Cove. Keeping our fingers crossed that the wind continues to blow the mosquitoes away, we proceed to happily dig ourselves a mess of clams. My good friend Dick Ames shared this recipe with me and I love it because it's so full of good clam and sausage flavor. *mg*

INGREDIENTS

20 QUAHOG CLAMS, AT LEAST 3 INCHES IN DIAMETER, OR 2 CUPS CHOPPED FRESH OR CANNED HARD-SHELL CLAMS, JUICES RESERVED

12 OUNCES ITALIAN SAUSAGE (COMBINATION OF SWEET AND HOT), REMOVED FROM CASINGS AND CRUMBLED

8 OUNCES CHORIZO SAUSAGE, ANY CASINGS REMOVED

8 TABLESPOONS (1 STICK) UNSALTED BUTTER

1 CUP FINELY DICED YELLOW ONION

1/2 CUP FINELY DICED GREEN BELL PEPPER

1/2 CUP FINELY DICED CELERY

3 CUPS LIGHTLY SEASONED CRUSHED BREAD STUFFING MIX, PLUS ADDITIONAL IF NECESSARY (SEE NOTES)

AT LEAST 1/2 CUP RESERVED CLAM BROTH OR DRAINED CLAM JUICES

MAKES 35 TO 40 STUFFED CLAMS

1. If using clams in the shell, rinse them several times until free of any sand and put in a large saucepan. Add cold water to a depth of 2 inches. Cover the pan tightly and steam over high heat for 4 to 5 minutes, or until the clams open. Drain the clams and discard any that do not open. Reserve the steaming liquid.

2. Let the clams cool slightly, then remove the meat from the shells. Reserve the clamshells.

3. Transfer the clam meat to a food processor fitted with the metal blade and pulse until chopped. (If using purchased chopped clams, chop them finer in the food processor.)

4. In a large, preferably nonstick skillet, brown the Italian sausage over medium heat, breaking up with a wooden spoon into small chunks, about 10 minutes. Cut the chorizo into 1/2-inch lengths and pulse in a food processor until finely chopped. Add the chorizo to the skillet and cook, stirring, for another 3 minutes. Scrape the sausage into a bowl, leaving the drippings in the pan.

5. Add the butter to the skillet and melt over medium-high heat. Add the onion, pepper, and celery and cook, stirring, for about 5 minutes, or until the vegetables soften. Add the 3 cups of stuffing mix, the chopped clams, the cooked sausage, and 1/2 cup reserved clam broth or juice. Use a large spoon or your hands to mix well, adding more bread crumbs or liquid as necessary to make a mixture that holds together when squeezed.

6. Lightly pack the clamshells with stuffing and place on baking sheets. Any leftover stuffing can be frozen. (Clams can be made a day ahead. Cover and refrigerate.)

7. Preheat the oven to 350 degrees.

8. Cover the baking sheets with foil and bake for 20 minutes. Remove the foil and continue to bake until the stuffing is lightly browned, 10 to 20 more minutes.

Notes

I use Pepperidge Farm stuffing mix for the bread crumbs.

You will need some clamshells for this dish. I have a bunch that I save from year to year just so I'll have them for stuffed clams.

If you're not starting with fresh clams in the shell, you can use a pint of chopped fresh hard-shell clams in juice that are sold in the seafood department of most supermarkets.

CRANBERRY-ORANGE JELL-O SHOTS

OUR EDITOR DEMANDED THAT we put this recipe in the book and gave us the following reason: "Years ago, when I visited you for the first time on Isle au Haut and stepped off the mailboat, I wasn't quite sure what I had gotten myself into. I was going to spend four days on an island with an author I didn't yet know well and her entire extended family. And there you all were, on the dock, greeting me with trays of Jell-O shots—and instantly I became part of this great extended family. So Jell-O shots will always symbolize for me Greenlaw hospitality. And that's why, even though they aren't really authentic Maine cuisine, I insist they be in this book." *lg*

INGREDIENTS

ONE 3-OUNCE PACKAGE CRANBERRY GELATIN

1 CUP ORANGE VODKA OR 1/2 CUP ORANGE VODKA AND 1/2 CUP RUM

MAKES 20

Pour the gelatin into a large bowl. Add 1 cup boiling water and stir until the gelatin dissolves. Stir in the vodka (or vodka and rum) and divide among twenty 1-ounce disposable paper cups. Refrigerate until firm, 2 to 4 hours.

NO, THESE ARE NOT MAINE SHRIMP.

MAINE SHRIMP REMOULADE

WHEN SMALL MAINE SHRIMP are in season in the winter I use them in all kinds of ways. This is a wonderful first course. The sauce is simple, delicious, and can be made ahead, and it makes a very pretty presentation. *mg*

REMOULADE SAUCE

2 CUPS MAYONNAISE

1 GARLIC CLOVE, MINCED OR PUT THROUGH A PRESS

1 HARD-COOKED EGG, CHOPPED

2 TABLESPOONS DRAINED CAPERS

1 TABLESPOON DIJON MUSTARD

1 TABLESPOON CHOPPED FRESH TARRAGON OR
1 TEASPOON DRIED

1 TABLESPOON CHOPPED FRESH CHERVIL OR
1 TEASPOON DRIED

1 TABLESPOON CHOPPED PARSLEY

SALT AND FRESHLY GROUND BLACK PEPPER

SALAD

2 POUNDS MAINE SHRIMP (SEE NOTE)

SHREDDED ROMAINE OR ICEBERG LETTUCE

PARSLEY OR OTHER HERB SPRIGS

SERVES 6 TO 8 AS A FIRST COURSE

1. Make the sauce. In a large bowl, whisk together the mayonnaise, garlic, chopped egg, capers, mustard, tarragon, chervil, and parsley. Season with salt and pepper to taste. Refrigerate for at least 1 hour or up to 2 days.

2. For the shrimp, bring a large pot of salted water to the boil. Add the shrimp and cook, stirring once or twice, for about 2 minutes, until the shrimp turn pink. Remove with a slotted spoon and transfer to a large bowl of ice water. Drain, peel off the shells, and remove any black veins. Chill until ready to use, up to 12 hours.

3. When ready to serve, line a large serving platter or individual plates with lettuce. Arrange the shrimp on the lettuce, spoon the sauce over the shrimp, garnish with herb sprigs, and serve.

Note

You can also buy shrimp already shelled, deveined, and/or cooked.

Any other type of shrimp can substitute for small Maine shrimp.

ROBINSON COVE CRAB SPREAD

ROBINSON COVE, named for my husband's family, is on the west side of Isle au Haut. When Jim was a boy he spent all of his summers at the old family homestead in the cove with his parents, sister, and three brothers. Mattie, Jim's mother, often made this simple and utterly delicious crab spread. I like it because it really showcases our sweet local crabmeat. *mg*

INGREDIENTS

12 OUNCES FRESH CRABMEAT, PICKED OVER

3/4 CUP REGULAR OR REDUCED-FAT MAYONNAISE

1/4 CUP SNIPPED CHIVES (SEE NOTE)

3 TABLESPOONS LEMON JUICE

2 TABLESPOONS PREPARED HORSERADISH

SALT AND FRESHLY GROUND BLACK PEPPER

ASSORTED DELICATE CRACKERS OR SMALL SLICES OF BREAD

SERVES 6 TO 8 AS AN HORS D'OEUVRE

1. In a medium-sized bowl, combine the crabmeat with the mayonnaise, chives, lemon juice, and horseradish. Mix well with a large fork to break up any larger chunks of crabmeat. Season with salt and pepper to taste. Refrigerate for up to 6 hours.
2. Serve in a bowl surrounded by crackers.

— *Note* —

If chives are unavailable, substitute finely chopped scallion.

HOT CRAB AND JALAPEÑO DIP

I CAN'T EVEN SAY THE WORD *jalapeño* without my eyes watering. But my son-in-law Ben adores spicy food—the hotter the better—so I made this hot crab and jalapeño dip one night with him in mind. So what does he do when I put it out on the table but head for the refrigerator to get some Tabasco sauce! By the time he polished off most of the dip I think we saw steam coming out of his ears. Personally, it's plenty hot enough for me (and probably for most) just the way it is. *mg*

INGREDIENTS

1/3 CUP SLICED ALMONDS

2 TABLESPOONS VEGETABLE OIL

1 LARGE RED BELL PEPPER, CHOPPED MEDIUM-FINE

1 1/2 TO 2 CUPS MAYONNAISE

1 CUP GRATED PARMESAN CHEESE

TWO 6-OUNCE JARS MARINATED ARTICHOKES, DRAINED AND CHOPPED FINE

1/2 CUP THINLY SLICED SCALLIONS

3 FRESH OR PICKLED JALAPEÑO PEPPERS, SEEDED AND MINCED (SEE NOTE)

4 TEASPOONS WORCESTERSHIRE SAUCE

2 TEASPOONS LEMON JUICE

1 TEASPOON CELERY SALT

1 POUND FRESH CRABMEAT, PICKED OVER

ASSORTED CRACKERS

SERVES ABOUT 10 AS AN HORS D'OEUVRE

1. In a medium skillet, toast the almonds over medium heat, stirring frequently, until one shade darker, 3 to 4 minutes. Remove and set aside.

2. In the same skillet, heat the oil. Add the red pepper and cook over medium-high heat, stirring frequently, until it begins to soften. Scrape into a large bowl.

3. Add 1 1/2 cups of the mayonnaise, the cheese, chopped artichokes, scallions, jalapeños, Worcestershire, lemon juice, and celery salt. Stir well to combine. Add the crabmeat and stir gently so as not to break up the crab chunks too much. If the mixture is too dry, stir in the additional 1/2 cup mayonnaise.

4. Butter an attractive ovenproof dish, transfer the crab mixture to it, and sprinkle with the toasted almonds. (The dish can be made up to 12 hours ahead and refrigerated. Return to room temperature before baking.)

5. Preheat the oven to 375 degrees.

6. Bake the crab dip, uncovered, until the mixture is hot and bubbly, 20 to 30 minutes. Spread on crackers to serve.

Note

Chopping jalapeño peppers can be seriously irritating to the eyes. Wash your hands thoroughly afterwards or wear rubber gloves when working with them. If you want a spicier dip, mince the jalapeño seeds and add to the mixture.

CRAB MADELEINES

THESE ARE A TRULY WONDERFUL AND very impressive hors d'oeuvre, but you do need French madeleine tins in order to make them. The molds, which you can find at specialty gourmet shops, are similar to muffin tins, but the pockets are in the shape of pretty scallop shells. *mg*

INGREDIENTS

2 TABLESPOONS CLARIFIED BUTTER (SEE NOTE)

1/2 CUP CAKE FLOUR

1/4 TEASPOON SALT

1/8 TEASPOON WHITE PEPPER

1/8 TEASPOON CAYENNE PEPPER

2 LARGE EGGS

6 TABLESPOONS GRATED PARMESAN CHEESE

6 OUNCES FRESH CRABMEAT (1 CUP), PICKED OVER AND FLAKED FINE

3 TABLESPOONS BUTTER, MELTED

2 TEASPOONS LEMON JUICE

CITRUS TARTAR SAUCE (PAGE 90),

REMOULADE SAUCE (PAGE 23), OR SALSA

SERVES 6 TO 8 (ABOUT 20 MADELEINES)

1. Brush the pockets of the madeleine tins thoroughly with the clarified butter. Refrigerate while making the batter. Preheat the oven to 350 degrees.

2. In a small bowl, whisk together the flour, salt, white pepper, and cayenne and set aside.

3. In a large bowl, using an electric mixer, beat the eggs on high speed until they are thick and pale yellow, about 2 minutes. Add the cheese and beat for 1 minute. Beat in the crabmeat.

4. Sprinkle the flour mixture over the egg mixture and whisk in gently but thoroughly, alternating with the melted butter. Stir in the lemon juice.

5. Spoon the batter into the madeleine tins, filling about three-quarters full. Bake in the preheated oven until golden brown and springy to the touch, 18 to 20 minutes. Unmold onto a rack to cool, loosening with the point of a small knife if necessary. Cool the molds, wipe clean, rebutter them, and repeat with the remaining batter. (These can be made a day ahead and stored, well wrapped, in the refrigerator. Arrange on a baking sheet and reheat in a 375-degree oven for about 5 minutes before serving.)

6. Serve with your favorite dipping sauce.

— *Note* —

To clarify butter, melt the butter and pour the clear yellow liquid off the top into a small bowl, leaving the milky residue behind. Using the clear liquid to butter the molds helps prevent the madeleines from sticking.

MUSSELS AU GRATIN

AT LOW TIDE WE CAN PICK MUSSELS off the rocks and ledges in front of our house. Although  these wild mussels are free, they do require a bit of work. You must first soak them in several changes of cold water, pull off their wiry beards, and scrub the shells. Our friend Dave Hiltz has been cultivating mussels that hang on ropes on his float in the harbor, and since these farmed mussels have never touched the sandy/muddy bottom they require little cleaning or scrubbing. This is a great way to serve them. *mg*

INGREDIENTS

3 POUNDS MUSSELS, SCRUBBED AND DEBEARDED (SEE HEADNOTE)

1 CUP WHITE WINE

1/2 CUP (1 STICK) UNSALTED BUTTER, MELTED

1/2 CUP BREAD CRUMBS

1/2 CUP GRATED PARMESAN CHEESE

3 TABLESPOONS CHOPPED PARSLEY

1 GARLIC CLOVE, CRUSHED IN A PRESS OR MINCED

1/2 TEASPOON FRESHLY GROUND BLACK PEPPER

SERVES 6 AS AN HORS D'OEUVRE

1. Place the mussels in a large pot, add the wine, and bring to a boil. Cover, reduce the heat to medium, and cook just until the mussels open, 5 to 10 minutes, depending on size. Lift the mussels out of the cooking liquid with a slotted spoon, transfer to a bowl, and reserve the cooking liquid. Discard the top shell of each of the mussels. If the mussels are small, place two in each remaining half shell; otherwise leave one per shell. Arrange on a rimmed baking sheet and drizzle with the melted butter.

2. In a small bowl, combine the crumbs, Parmesan, parsley, garlic, and pepper and sprinkle the mixture over the mussels. Drizzle with a little of the reserved cooking liquid. (The mussels can be prepared ahead to this point and refrigerated or held at cool room temperature for a couple of hours.)

3. Preheat the oven to 400 degrees.

4. Place the baking sheet in the oven and cook until the mussels are hot and bubbly, about 10 minutes. Turn the setting to broil and cook, about 5 inches from the heating element, until nicely browned on top, 1 to 2 minutes.

PENOBSCOT BAY CLAM DIP

WE BUILT OUR RETIREMENT HOME on the island sixteen years ago, and when the last nail was pounded in we put up a notice in the town post office inviting all to an open house on the following Saturday. Everyone on the island loves a party, and eighty neighbors showed up, including kids and dogs! We ate, drank, and talked the afternoon away. One of the items on the buffet was this clam dip and I wrapped the loaf of bread in a red bandanna, which made it look very festive. Our friend and fellow lobsterman Greg Runge stood right next to that clam dip for most of the afternoon! *mg*

INGREDIENTS

1 LARGE ROUND LOAF CRUSTY FRENCH BREAD
(ABOUT 24 OUNCES)

TWO 8-OUNCE PACKAGES CREAM CHEESE, SOFTENED

1 1/2 CUPS MINCED CLAMS, 1/4 CUP JUICE RESERVED

2 TABLESPOONS GRATED ONION

2 TABLESPOONS BEER (OPTIONAL)

2 TEASPOONS WORCESTERSHIRE SAUCE

2 TEASPOONS LEMON JUICE

1 TEASPOON HOT PEPPER SAUCE, OR TO TASTE

1/2 TEASPOON SALT

1 TABLESPOON CHOPPED PARSLEY

RAW VEGETABLES FOR DIPPING, SUCH AS BABY CARROTS, GRAPE TOMATOES, PEPPER STRIPS, CELERY STICKS

SERVES 12 OR MORE AS AN HORS D'OEUVRE

1. With a sharp knife, slice the top off the bread and set aside. Hollow out the loaf, leaving about a 1-inch-thick shell.

2. In a large bowl, beat the cream cheese with the clams, onion, optional beer, Worcestershire sauce, lemon juice, hot pepper sauce, salt, and reserved clam juice.

3. Preheat the oven to 250 degrees. Cut two long sheets of aluminum foil and crisscross them on a baking sheet. Center the hollowed loaf on the foil, fill with the clam mixture, and place the top on the bread. Wrap in foil.

4. Bake for 3 hours to blend the flavors and until the dip is piping hot. Remove the top, sprinkle the dip with parsley, and place on a large platter. Surround with raw vegetables for dipping.

> **Notes**
>
> You can use finely chopped fresh clams, or three 6 1/2-ounce cans of minced clams.
>
> The beer is a nice addition, but I only use it if the rest of the bottle is not going to go to waste!
>
> If you like, cut the removed bread into cubes, toast for about 20 minutes in the slow oven, and serve along with the vegetables for dipping.

MUSSELS ON THE HALF-SHELL WITH TWO ASIAN SAUCES

ALTHOUGH DAD INSISTS that he taught Mom how to fry an egg, his culinary activity, to the best of my knowledge, has been somewhat sketchy. I do, however, have fond memories of Dad in the kitchen preparing mussels. In those days, eating mussels was not fashionable, and I questioned my parents as to why we were not eating clams like normal people. Dad explained that he had been eating the island mussels since he was a boy and he happened to like them at least as much as clams. *lg*

THAI CURRY SAUCE

1/2 CUP CANNED UNSWEETENED COCONUT MILK

1 TEASPOON THAI RED CURRY PASTE (SEE NOTE), OR MORE TO TASTE

3 TABLESPOONS FINELY DICED RED BELL PEPPER

SOY BUTTER

4 TABLESPOONS (1/2 STICK) UNSALTED BUTTER

2 TABLESPOONS SOY SAUCE

3 TABLESPOONS FINELY MINCED SCALLIONS

2 POUNDS MUSSELS, SCRUBBED AND DEBEARDED

SERVES 4 AS AN HORS D'OEUVRE

1. For the Thai Curry Sauce, combine the coconut milk and curry paste in a small saucepan. Bring to a boil, whisking, and simmer, uncovered, over medium heat for about 5 minutes, until slightly reduced and thickened.

2. For the Soy Butter, combine the butter and soy sauce in a small saucepan. Simmer for about 2 minutes over medium heat until blended.

3. Place the mussels in a large pot. Add about 1/4 cup of water and bring to a boil. Cover, reduce the heat to medium, and cook just until the shells open, 5 to 10 minutes, depending on size. Discard the top shell of each of the mussels and place a cooked mussel in each of the remaining shells. Arrange on two baking sheets. Spoon about a teaspoon of the Thai Curry Sauce over half the mussels; spoon the Soy Butter over the remaining half. (The mussels can be prepared ahead to this point and refrigerated or held at cool room temperature for a couple of hours.)

4. Preheat the oven to 400 degrees.

5. Place the baking sheets in the oven and cook until the mussels are hot and the sauce is bubbly, about 10 minutes.

6. Sprinkle the Thai curry mussels with the minced red pepper, sprinkle the soy mussels with the chopped scallions, and serve.

Note

You'll find Thai curry paste in jars or sealed pouches in the Asian section of most supermarkets. It varies in intensity, so use according to your own taste.

WHISKEY FRUIT PUNCH

THE FIRST TIME I TRIED THIS PUNCH I didn't realize what a "punch" it had! It is a good-tasting, slow-sipping holiday drink. My advice: lots of ice! *mg*

INGREDIENTS

2 CUPS SUGAR

2 CUPS BREWED TEA

2 CUPS WHITE OR PURPLE GRAPE JUICE

2 CUPS PINEAPPLE JUICE

2 CUPS ORANGE JUICE

1 CUP LEMON JUICE

1 QUART GINGER ALE

1 CUP MARASCHINO CHERRIES, JUICE AND ALL

1 QUART RYE WHISKEY

MAKES 1 1/2 GALLONS OR ABOUT 48 1/2-CUP SERVINGS

1. In a 2-gallon punch bowl or other container, combine the sugar and tea and stir well. Add the grape juice, pineapple juice, orange juice, and lemon juice and stir to combine. Let stand for at least 30 minutes or until the sugar is completely dissolved.

2. When ready to serve, add the ginger ale, cherries, and whiskey and stir to combine. Add ice cubes and use a ladle to serve into small cups.

WHALER'S TODDY

THE VERY NAME OF THIS WARMING TODDY makes me think of old whaling ships coming into port in the dead of a cold night. Maybe people on the dock are waiting to catch their lines and the crew disembarks and heads to the nearest tavern for a hot toddy. In today's world it would certainly be a welcome libation after a long afternoon on the ski slopes. *mg*

INGREDIENTS

2 OUNCES DARK RUM

1 TEASPOON BROWN SUGAR OR MOLASSES

3 WHOLE CLOVES

1 LEMON SLICE

BOILING WATER

CINNAMON STICK

SERVES 1

In a heavy mug, combine the rum, brown sugar or molasses, cloves, and lemon slice. Add enough boiling water to fill the mug, stir to blend with the cinnamon stick, and serve.

─ *Note* ─

To make sure the mug is really warm, heat it by standing it in a pan of water on the stove. Bring the water to a slow boil and then make the toddy.

SWEET AND SPICY ROASTED NUTS

I OFTEN MAKE THESE NUTS for our holiday parties. As they are somewhat addictive, I find I need to hide them from myself so they don't disappear before party night! They also make a perfect holiday or hostess gift packaged in an attractive jar and tied with a ribbon. *mg*

INGREDIENTS

6 TABLESPOONS (3/4 STICK) UNSALTED BUTTER

1/2 CUP PACKED LIGHT BROWN SUGAR

1 TABLESPOON CHILI POWDER

1 TEASPOON GROUND CUMIN

1 TEASPOON DRIED OREGANO

1 TEASPOON SALT

1/2 TEASPOON FRESHLY GROUND BLACK PEPPER

1/4 TEASPOON CAYENNE PEPPER

2 CUPS WALNUT HALVES

2 CUPS PECAN HALVES

2 CUPS WHOLE ALMONDS

MAKES 6 CUPS

1. Preheat the oven to 300 degrees. Spray a large baking sheet with vegetable oil spray.
2. In a large skillet, melt the butter. Add the sugar, 1/4 cup water, the chili powder, cumin, oregano, salt, black pepper, and cayenne. Cook over medium heat, stirring, until the sugar dissolves, about 3 minutes. Add the nuts and cook, stirring, until the butter mixture coats the nuts evenly, about 2 minutes. Scrape onto the prepared baking sheet and spread out evenly in a single layer.
3. Bake in the preheated oven, stirring every few minutes, until the nuts are glazed and deep brown, about 25 minutes. Cool completely on the baking sheet, stirring occasionally. Store in a covered container at room temperature for up to a week.

MUSHROOM TURNOVERS

ALTHOUGH THESE ARE KIND OF FIDDLY, they're worth the work. They can be made ahead, and guests love them! You can use almost any type of mushrooms for the filling, and now that such a wide variety of wild mushrooms are available in the supermarket I often use a combination of several for these turnovers. *mg*

INGREDIENTS

2 TABLESPOONS (1/4 STICK) UNSALTED BUTTER

1/2 CUP FINELY CHOPPED YELLOW ONION

6 OUNCES MUSHROOMS

1 TEASPOON FLOUR

1/2 TEASPOON DRIED THYME

1/2 TEASPOON SALT

PINCH OF CAYENNE PEPPER

ONE 15-OUNCE PACKAGE REFRIGERATED PIE CRUST (2 ROUNDS), OR 1 RECIPE FLAKY PIE CRUST (PAGE 226)

1 LARGE EGG BEATEN WITH 1 TABLESPOON WATER

MAKES ABOUT 32 SMALL TURNOVERS

1. For the filling, heat the butter in a large skillet. Add the onion and cook over medium heat until softened.

2. In a food processor fitted with a steel blade, pulse the mushrooms until they are finely chopped. You should have about 1 1/2 cups. Add the mushrooms to the skillet and cook, stirring frequently, until most of the liquid evaporates, about 5 minutes. Sprinkle on the flour and thyme and cook, stirring, for 1 minute. Season with salt and pepper. Refrigerate until completely cool.

3. Using a 2 1/2-inch cookie cutter, cut rounds out of rolled-out pastry. Place 1 teaspoon of mushroom filling on the upper half of each round and brush the edge with the egg wash. Fold over and pinch the edges to seal. Place on a baking sheet and brush with more egg glaze. (The turnovers can be refrigerated for several hours or frozen.)

4. Preheat the oven to 375 degrees.

5. Bake the turnovers for 12 to 15 minutes, or until the pastry is golden brown. Serve warm.

WALNUT SALAD IN ENDIVE

THERE'S SOMETHING about this particular combination of ingredients that makes people think they are eating something more substantial than toasted nuts. Everyone loves this appetizer, and many have offered guesses as to what they are tasting—and have never been right. *lg*

INGREDIENTS

1 CUP WALNUTS

1 CUP SHREDDED PARMESAN CHEESE

1/2 CUP FINELY CHOPPED CELERY

2 TABLESPOONS LEMON JUICE

1 TABLESPOON MAYONNAISE, PLUS ADDITIONAL IF NECESSARY

2 TEASPOONS OLIVE OIL

1 GARLIC CLOVE, CRUSHED THROUGH A PRESS OR FINELY CHOPPED

1/2 TEASPOON SALT, OR TO TASTE

FRESHLY GROUND BLACK PEPPER

4 ENDIVES

1/4 CUP CHOPPED FLAT-LEAF PARSLEY

SERVES ABOUT 6 AS AN HORS D'OEUVRE

1. Preheat the oven to 350 degrees.
2. Spread the walnuts onto a baking sheet and toast in the oven, stirring once or twice, until one shade darker, about 10 minutes. Cool and finely chop in a food processor or by hand with a large knife. Reserve the walnuts.
3. In a bowl, combine the cheese, celery, lemon juice, mayonnaise, olive oil, garlic, salt, and pepper to taste. (The mixture can be made to this point and refrigerated overnight.)
4. Trim the endives and separate into leaves.
5. Add the walnuts and parsley to the cheese mixture, adding more mayonnaise if the mixture seems too dry. Season to taste. Spoon about a teaspoon of the walnut mixture onto the wide end of the endive leaves, arrange on a platter, and serve.

WIMPY SUSHI FOR THOSE WITH AN AVERSION TO RAW FISH

I HAVE ALWAYS ENJOYED OYSTERS and clams and even scallops raw, but was late to come to an appreciation of other seafood served uncooked. My boyfriend, who still remembers lessons from medical school, is squeamish and cannot stomach anything that is not cooked to a fare-thee-well, so this recipe allows us to enjoy sushi together. *lg*

INGREDIENTS

1 POUND SUSHI-GRADE AHI TUNA STEAK

2 TEASPOONS VEGETABLE OIL

2 CUPS COOKED AND COOLED SUSHI RICE (SEE NOTE)

1 OR 2 THIN EUROPEAN CUCUMBERS, UNPEELED AND SLICED ABOUT 1/4 INCH THICK, OR 3 HEADS ENDIVE, SEPARATED INTO LEAVES

ABOUT 1/4 CUP WASABI PASTE

ABOUT 1/2 CUP PICKLED GINGER

ABOUT 1/2 CUP SNIPPED CHIVES

ABOUT 1/2 CUP LIGHT SOY SAUCE

SERVES ABOUT 6 AS AN HORS D'OEUVRE

1. Preheat a gas grill or barbecue fire to hot. Rub the tuna with oil and grill to your liking, 2 to 3 minutes for medium rare. Cool the tuna and cut into thin slices, then into bite-sized pieces.

2. Place a rounded teaspoon of rice onto a cucumber slice or endive leaf. Top the ball of rice with a piece of tuna, a dab of wasabi, a piece of pickled ginger, and a few chives. Repeat until you run out of something. Drizzle with a small amount of soy or pass it as a dipping sauce.

Note

Sushi rice is short-grain Japanese rice. Cook it following the package directions. It can usually be found with other Asian ingredients—wasabi, pickled ginger, and the like—in the Asian foods section of most supermarkets.

DARK AND STORMY

I HAVE TO ADMIT THAT my first Dark and Stormy did little to impress me. It was served as a "welcome aboard" libation upon boarding a visiting sailboat in the Isle au Haut thoroughfare. Two friends and I were handed large plastic beer mugs filled to the brim with a brownish beverage. A chronic problem with yacht drinks is a shortage of ice, and my first encounter with this cocktail was no exception, as the bartender had been stingy with cubes and generous with rum. After one sip, Patti and Doug looked frantically around the cockpit for a plant to water. Being the heartier sailor of the three, I was able to choke mine down, trying to avoid swallowing the tired wedge of lime that drifted aimlessly in the sea of booze. The next Dark and Stormy I drank was made with perfect proportions and it has become one of my favorite cocktails. *lg*

INGREDIENTS

4 OUNCES DARK RUM (I LIKE GOSLING'S, WHICH IS MADE IN BERMUDA)

12 OUNCES GINGER BEER

FRESH LIME WEDGES

SERVES 2

Place some ice cubes in two medium-sized glasses. Add rum and ginger beer and stir to blend well. Garnish each drink with a wedge of lime and serve.

STEPHANIE'S HOLIDAY CHEESE BALL

MANY PEOPLE LIKE TO SERVE CHEESE BALLS at holiday parties, and I think this recipe is a particularly delicious combination of cheeses and seasonings. My dear friend Stephanie brought it for our Christmas Eve gathering one year and I've been making it ever since. *mg*

INGREDIENTS

1/2 CUP WALNUTS

1 POUND CREAM CHEESE, SOFTENED

6 OUNCES BLUE CHEESE, CRUMBLED

1 TABLESPOON MEDIUM-DRY SHERRY

1 TEASPOON WORCESTERSHIRE SAUCE

15 PIMIENTO-STUFFED OLIVES, COARSELY CHOPPED

CRACKERS, FOR SERVING

MAKES 1 LARGE OR 2 SMALLER BALLS, SERVING ABOUT 10

1. Toast the nuts in a dry skillet over medium heat, stirring frequently, until one shade darker, about 4 minutes. Remove to a cutting board and finely chop.

2. In a food processor, combine the cream cheese, blue cheese, sherry, and Worcestershire. Pulse until the mixture is well blended. (Or blend by hand in a large bowl.) Transfer to a bowl, add the olives, and blend. Shape the mixture into one large or two smaller balls, roll in the nuts, and chill. (The cheese ball can be made up to 2 days ahead.)

3. Remove the ball from the refrigerator an hour or so before ready to serve. Place on a platter, surround with crackers, and serve.

CHAPTER 2
LOBSTER, CRAB, AND OTHER SHELLFISH

ISLE AU HAUT PLAIN STEAMED OR BOILED LOBSTER

TO BOIL OR TO STEAM? That is the question. I steam new-shelled lobsters (soft-shell or shedders) and boil hard-shells. Lobsters that have recently shed or molted have room to grow between the meat and shell and this space is filled with seawater, so new-shells are actually cooking in their own water. Since hard-shelled lobsters can be dried out by steaming, I like to boil them. We're often cooking for a lot of people, so I have rigged up a good system on my deck for cooking the lobsters, which consists of a big turkey frying kettle set on a propane burner. *lg*

INGREDIENTS

FOUR 1 1/2-POUND SOFT-SHELL LOBSTERS

1/4 POUND (1 STICK) SALTED BUTTER, MELTED

SERVES 4

1. In a large kettle, bring 3 inches of water to a rolling boil. Plunge the lobsters into the pot, cover, return to the boil, and cook for about 15 minutes, or until the lobsters turn bright red. Drain, split the tails with a large knife if desired, and place a lobster on each serving plate.
2. Divide the butter into four small dishes and serve with the lobsters for dipping.
3. To eat a lobster, first twist off the claws. Crack each claw with a nutcracker, hammer, or anything handy, and push the meat out with your finger or a pick.
4. Bend the tail back and twist to remove it from the body. Break off the flippers from the end of the tail and suck out any meat. Use a fork or your thumb to push the meat out of the tail. Discard the back intestinal vein before eating the meat.
5. Break off the small claws and suck the meat out. They are excellent eating.
6. Break open the body and pick out any small tidbits of meat along the sides. And don't miss the tomalley, or liver. It turns green when cooked and is considered a delicacy by many lobster eaters.

> *Note*
>
> To cook hard-shells, bring a large pot of water to the boil. Plunge lobsters into the water, cover, return to the boil, and cook as above for about 15 minutes.

AUNT HARRIET'S CRABMEAT QUICHE

THIS RECIPE WAS SHARED WITH ME by Grace Leeman and Harriet Huff of Orr's Island, Maine (ages eighty-five and ninety-two, respectively, and known as the Thelma and Louise of their island), and if they say it's good, it's good! *lg*

INGREDIENTS

1 CUP SHREDDED MILD CHEDDAR CHEESE

ONE UNBAKED 9-INCH PIE SHELL (SEE FLAKY PIE CRUST, PAGE 226 OR USE PURCHASED CRUST)

8 OUNCES CRABMEAT, PICKED OVER TO REMOVE ANY SHELL OR CARTILAGE

2 SMALL YELLOW ONIONS, FINELY CHOPPED

3 EGGS

1 CUP LIGHT CREAM

1/2 TEASPOON SALT

1/4 TEASPOON DRY MUSTARD

1 TABLESPOON CHOPPED PARSLEY

SERVES 4

1. Preheat the oven to 325 degrees.
2. Sprinkle the cheese into the bottom of the prepared pie shell and top with the crabmeat and chopped onions.
3. In a medium bowl, lightly beat the eggs and whisk in the cream, salt, and mustard. Pour the custard mixture over the crabmeat and sprinkle with parsley.
4. Bake in the preheated oven until a small knife inserted two-thirds of the way to the center comes out clean, about 45 minutes. Cool for at least 15 minutes before cutting into wedges to serve.

The Beginner's Guide to Clambakes
or How to Ruin a Perfectly Good Lobster

I COULDN'T FIND A SATISFACTORY DEFINITION in Webster's, so I have defined "clambake" myself. *CLAMBAKE: The act of, and all activity surrounding, the cooking of certain shellfishes over open fires at the ocean's edge.*

"Cooking in a washtub" is New England's way of saying that a crowd is expected for dinner. But other than at a good old-fashioned clambake, I am not aware of any time when a washtub is actually used in food preparation in spite of the expression indicating otherwise. The washtub itself is ideally suited for the task of clambaking in that its original design and use were intended for laundering clothes, and not at all for steaming clams or boiling lobster. Clams are not baked at clambakes (at least not the ones I have attended), and I assume the term comes from a day when things were buried in a pit with hot coals to be dug up days later and consumed. Somewhere along the line, someone discovered a better way (not much better), probably about the time of the invention of the wringer washing machine, and the new method of clambaking was the answer to the question "What the hell will we do with the washtub?"

In preparation for a clambake, the following will be needed: lobsters, clams, corn on the cob, butter, hot dogs, marshmallows, two huge galvanized washtubs—one for the corn and one for the shellfish—firewood, several cases of beer, and as many ill-behaved children as you can find.

The first, and perhaps most critical, step toward a successful clambake is choosing the right location. Theories vary on this, but in my experience it is proper to choose a spot along the beach that is most uncomfortable. Make sure that your selected site meets at least two of the following criteria:

1. There is absolutely nowhere to sit down.
2. The beach is comprised of round rocks that shift when stepped on to ensure poor footing.
3. There are sheer, jagged cliffs in the area for children to play on.

4. The immediate area is void of driftwood so that burning material has to be dragged some distance.

5. You are in view of at least one neighbor who will report you to the fire warden for "burning without a permit."

Once you have selected the most inconvenient location, you need to think about timing and consider things like when you would like to eat, darkness, and high tide.

So the planning stage is complete. Now it's time to drink beer. Hopefully you were wise (cheap) enough to bring only canned beer, as glass can be hazardous under these circumstances. So, crack open the first can of whatever you are drinking and remind everyone else that you were an Eagle Scout or Campfire Girl and therefore you will be in charge of building the fires. It is alright to be a bit obnoxious in bossing your friends and family around. After all, your attitude may be what ensures that clambakes do not become annual events in your life.

Now that you have taken charge and delegated everything that resembles work, relax and drink another beer while your guests collect, drag, lug, and pile driftwood and other debris from the surrounding area. When you determine that an adequate pile of combustibles has been gathered, go ahead and get the fires started. You'll need one fire for each washtub of food to be cooked. (For a group of thirty or less, two fires should be sufficient.) Feel free to burn the entire stack of paper plates to get the wood going as paper plates are otherwise useless at a clambake.

Once the fires are burning strong, manhandle a few large rocks around their perimeters in such a way that the washtubs may soon sit upon them and over the flames. Dip each washtub into the ocean to collect some saltwater. There is no science to the amount—"some" is what you will end up with after carrying the washtub from the edge of the water, over slippery ledges and craggy rocks, and back to the fires. Place the tubs of water over the fires and wait for the water to boil. If you did not spill much along the way, this could take a long time. Drink more beer.

While waiting for the water to boil is a good time to take stock of the situation and evaluate the day thus far. I use a simple checklist like the following:

1. Has anyone sprained an ankle yet?

2. Have we run out of beer?

3. Is anyone bitching about the mosquitoes or the temperature?

4. Are at least two children in "time out"?

5. Has anyone suggested that the rising tide may douse the fires before the food even begins to cook? If you do not answer "yes" to at least three of these queries, know that you are not having a true clambake experience.

When your pals confirm that "the friggin' water is finally boiling," it is time to put the food in. It's usually a little toasty and very smoky close to the fires, so you'll probably need to stand back and toss things into the tubs. This can be considered a game of sorts and you may allow others to join in. Toss the lobsters first as they take the longest to cook. Next, toss the corn into its tub. Do not toss clams at this time. Throw heaps of wet seaweed over the tops of the washtubs now cooking the lobster and corn. The seaweed serves as a cover to keep the heat from escaping.

By now the children are getting cranky. Although you suggest ignoring or spanking, their parents insist on feeding them. At this point everyone should go off in search of sticks or branches onto which to skewer hot dogs and marshmallows to roast over the fires, leaving you to tend to the adult fare. Before the search party returns, you decide to add the clams to the top of the lobster tub and do so by pulling back the seaweed cover with whatever you can find to protect your hands from the steam. Choose regardless of ownership and expensive appearance.

The children are the quietest they have been all day and are delighted to be allowed to play with fire. They do not actually eat anything, but the adults do not notice as they are busy arguing about how long the lobsters have been cooking. The children continue to amuse themselves with marshmallow torches until the last flaming sugar ball blackens, slides off the scorched end of a stick, and onto the top of a bare foot. A bit of screeching ensues and while everyone else consoles the victim, you declare, "The bugs are done," and wonder what to do about it. Others join you in calculating how best to remove the food from the fires without another third-degree burn. Someone, probably the teetotaler in the group, suggests using a large pole as a lever. You agree and manage to tip both washtubs over, spilling the contents onto the rocks to cool. If everything goes well, all of the guests will be convinced that you know exactly what you are doing. The steaming food will be displayed on top of the seaweed. Everything looks great!

The food is cool enough to handle when you realize that you have nothing in which to melt the butter. Do not attempt melting butter over red coals in a plastic, microwavable container. (I realize many readers are thinking, Duh! but you'd be surprised.) If smearing corn with a stick of butter does not provide enough fat and cholesterol for some folks, drawn butter can be made using half of an empty beer can. Be advised that this move risks cuts and burns to the fingers.

The feast begins. Be ready to field the inevitable question from the virgin clambaker as meat is pulled from the lobster's tail: "Is it supposed to be this color?"

"Yes" is always reassuring. Do not edit or ad-lib. Have fun! *lg*

BAKED STUFFED LOBSTER THE INN AT ISLE AU HAUT

SOMETHING REALLY GOOD HAPPENED on the island last summer. Dianna Santaspago opened a new inn on the east side and called it The Inn at Isle au Haut. Dianna is a fantastic cook and everyone who ate in her dining room that first summer agrees that not only is her food wonderful, but everything about the place—service, atmosphere, comfort level—is lovely. This is her baked stuffed lobster, and, like everything Dianna does, it has her special touch. *mg*

INGREDIENTS

1/4 POUND (1 STICK) UNSALTED BUTTER

3 TABLESPOONS FINELY CHOPPED SHALLOTS

2 GARLIC CLOVES, MINCED

1/4 CUP MEDIUM-DRY SHERRY

1 POUND FRESH CRABMEAT, PICKED OVER TO REMOVE ANY SHELL OR CARTILAGE

1 CUP CRUSHED RITZ CRACKERS

2 TABLESPOONS CHOPPED PARSLEY

SALT AND FRESHLY GROUND BLACK PEPPER

4 LIVE 1 1/2-POUND LOBSTERS

3 TABLESPOONS BUTTER, MELTED

SERVES 4

1. In a large sauté pan, melt the butter. Add the shallots and cook over medium heat, stirring, until beginning to soften. Add the garlic and cook for 1 minute. Add the sherry and cook for 1 minute. Remove from the heat and add the crabmeat, cracker crumbs, and parsley. Season to taste with salt and pepper. (You may not need salt because the cracker crumbs can be salty.) Cool the stuffing completely.

2. Preheat the oven to 425 degrees.

3. Place the lobsters on a cutting board and use a large knife to split them in half. Remove the sand sac from the head and the black intestinal vein. Take off the claw bands and, if the lobsters are hard-shells, crack the claws in a couple of places with a hammer so the heat will penetrate. Place the lobsters, cut sides up, on two rimmed baking sheets and sprinkle the stuffing mixture over the tail and bodies of the lobsters. Drizzle with melted butter.

4. Bake until the lobster meat is opaque and the crumbs are crisp and golden brown, 15 to 22 minutes.

Note

Splitting live lobsters takes a little getting used to, but after doing the first one it's pretty easy. You should not do this more than an hour ahead because the meat can begin to deteriorate once the lobsters are no longer alive.

BARTER CREEK CLAM CHOWDER

HALF THE FUN OF PUTTING TOGETHER a clam chowder is digging the clams. We are lucky to have several flats for clam digging on the island, including the one at Barter Creek, but clams are pretty readily available in seafood markets all over most of the rest of New England. If you think clams are expensive, try digging them yourself. Rewarding, yes, but it's backbreaking work. This is a very typical milky Maine-style chowder made with soft-shell (sometimes called "pisser") clams and not thickened with flour. *lg*

INGREDIENTS

1 1/2 POUNDS SOFT-SHELL CLAMS

3 BACON STRIPS, COARSELY CHOPPED

1 LARGE YELLOW ONION, CHOPPED
(I LIKE TO USE A VIDALIA OR OTHER SWEET ONION)

4 MEDIUM POTATOES, PEELED AND CUT INTO 3/4-INCH DICE

2 CUPS MILK

ONE 12-OUNCE CAN EVAPORATED MILK

1/2 CUP (1 STICK) UNSALTED BUTTER

2 TABLESPOONS CHOPPED PARSLEY

SALT AND FRESHLY GROUND BLACK PEPPER

SERVES 4 AS A MAIN COURSE

1. Scrub the clams well to remove any mud. Use a small sturdy knife to open, working over a bowl to save the juices. Discard the black neck skin and if they are too large to eat in a bite, cut into smaller pieces. Or steam the clams in about 1/2 cup water just until they begin to open, 5 to 8 minutes. Shuck, discarding the neck skin and cutting up if large. Reserve the broth, letting any sediment settle to the bottom of the pot.

2. In a large soup pot, cook the bacon over medium heat until crisp, about 10 minutes. Remove with a slotted spoon and reserve, leaving the bacon fat in the pot. Add the onion and cook until it begins to soften, about 5 minutes. Add the potatoes and enough water or a combination of water and clam broth to cover. Bring to a simmer, reduce the heat to medium-low, and cook until the potatoes are tender, about 15 minutes. Add the milk, evaporated milk, butter, and clams with any juices. Simmer over low heat until the butter melts and the clams are cooked, about 5 minutes. Add the reserved bacon (or sprinkle the bacon on top just before serving) and parsley and season with salt and pepper to taste. Serve immediately or cool and refrigerate overnight. Reheat gently.

LINDA & MARTHA GREENLAW

Clamming

FOUR EIGHT-INCH RUSTED TINES of the "clam hoe" are thrust into firm, cool flats with the anticipation of finding a single clam. "One hole, one clam," Aunt Gracie always assures as she walks slowly and methodically across the low-tide beach, head bent and scouting the next hole.

The sun feels good on my lower back, exposed between belt and T-shirt raised to the midriff as I hunch to dig the spot marked by the dragging of the scout's toe through wet sand. My sister, wading knee-deep in the incoming flood, which is warmed as it creeps across the suntanned shore, is in her favorite sand dollar place and teasingly notes my "Deer Isle smile," which nonclammers know as "plumber's crack." I straighten my back, pull my shirt down and pants up with sandy hands, and inspect the harvest freshly rinsed and shining white in the wooden basket at my feet.

"Do you think we have enough?" I ask my mother, knowing she'll say we are shy of some never-defined amount of clams for steaming. Mom's always the last to concede to the incoming tide that chases us slowly yet relentlessly ashore, nipping at our heels, flooding the newly dug trenches, and leveling mounds of turned flats, uncaring of the effort in creating such a ragged landscape. Aunt Gracie, still searching and scratching markers for the digger, confirms that we are indeed unfinished as she draws the toe of her sneaker from right to left, leaving a line in the sand and calling, "One hole, one clam."

With feet spread wide, I bend at the waist, push the tines deep with my left hand, then yank up on the gritty, wooden handle with my right and flip a fork full of sand back and between my legs like a center hiking a football. In the bottom of the hole a clam neck retracts and disappears. But not quickly enough. Excavating now with a bare hand, I push stiff fingers into the cold, wet sand where the neck was spied. I feel the sharp edges of a shell with my fingertips and wiggle my index finger and thumb deep enough to grasp the clam and pull it out of hiding. The perfect size. I admire the clam for a second, then toss it into the basket.

My niece has returned from her hunt for sea glass and proudly displays shards of ceramics and bits of old bottles, edges smooth and rounded by their time tumbling in the tide. The sand dollar collector displays her finds, too, and we agree that it's been a successful harvest all the way around. We move sand dollars, sea glass, and clams to escape the saltwater that is gaining ground, and crowd what's left of a narrow strip of flats pinched between water and ledge. Generations two and three are ready to head home while the first has discovered more holes. I tug the back of my jeans up once more and look for the next mark. *lg*

BATTER-FRIED CLAMS

DURING THE SUMMER I try my best to sample as many fried clams as possible at the dozens of seasonal clam shacks up and down the New England coast. Which is better—clams coated in batter or crumbs? Depends on a lot of factors, such as the freshness of the clams, the quality of the oil, and other things, but when everything is right I tend to prefer batter. If the clams are large, I like to "squeeze the bellies," which means pinching the belly to get the gross black goo out, but truthfully, by the time the clams are coated with batter and fried, you can't see the goo anymore and it really doesn't taste bad. *lg*

INGREDIENTS

2 POUNDS SMALL SOFT-SHELL CLAMS

1 3/4 CUPS ALL-PURPOSE FLOUR

1 TEASPOON BAKING SODA

1 TEASPOON SALT

1 CUP SOUR MILK (SEE NOTE)

1 LARGE EGG

VEGETABLE OIL FOR FRYING

SERVES 4

1. Shuck the clams. In a large bowl, whisk together the flour, baking soda, and salt. Whisk in the milk and egg to make a batter about the consistency of heavy cream.

2. Heat the oil in a deep fryer or heavy deep skillet to 365 degrees. Dip clams in the batter, letting any excess drip off, slide into the hot fat, and cook, turning once with tongs, until golden brown, 2 to 3 minutes. Drain on paper towels and serve hot.

Note

This old-fashioned recipe calls for sour milk, which, before the days of reliable refrigeration, used to be more common in the kitchen larder. To make it, add 2 teaspoons white or cider vinegar to a cup of milk and let stand for about 10 minutes to sour.

HEAD HARBOR LOBSTER & HADDOCK CASSEROLE

BEING MARRIED TO A LOBSTER FISHERMAN has many advantages, one of which is a plentiful supply of lobster meat. I have come to be known (not surprisingly, I guess) for my repertoire of lobster dishes. This mixed seafood casserole, chock full of chunks of beautiful lobster meat as well as haddock, is one of the best. *mg*

INGREDIENTS

2 POUNDS HADDOCK FILLETS

1/2 CUP (1 STICK) UNSALTED BUTTER

1/2 CUP ALL-PURPOSE FLOUR

3 CUPS HALF-AND-HALF

3 TABLESPOONS KETCHUP

1 TABLESPOON HORSERADISH

2 TEASPOONS DIJON MUSTARD

1 TABLESPOON LEMON JUICE

1 TABLESPOON WORCESTERSHIRE SAUCE

1/4 CUP MEDIUM-DRY SHERRY

4 TABLESPOONS CHOPPED PARSLEY

3/4 TEASPOON SALT, OR TO TASTE

1 POUND (ABOUT 3 CUPS) DICED COOKED LOBSTER MEAT

1 1/2 CUPS FRESH BREAD CRUMBS

2 TABLESPOONS BUTTER, MELTED

SERVES 10 TO 12

1. Butter a shallow 3-quart casserole dish.

2. Place the haddock in a skillet, add water to cover, bring to the simmer, and cook gently until the fish is no longer translucent in the center, 5 to 8 minutes. Remove with a slotted spoon to a bowl. When cool enough to handle, break the fish into small chunks.

3. In a large heavy saucepan or deep skillet, melt the butter. Add the flour and cook over medium to medium-high heat, whisking, for 2 minutes. Whisk in the half-and-half, bring to a boil, and cook, whisking for 1 minute. Whisk in the ketchup, horseradish, mustard, lemon juice, and Worcestershire and simmer for 2 to 3 minutes to blend the flavors. Whisk in the sherry and parsley and season with salt. The sauce will be very thick at this point; it will thin out with the addition of the seafood.

4. In a large bowl or in the pan, combine the haddock and lobster meat with the sauce. Taste for seasoning again and adjust if necessary. Transfer to the prepared dish, sprinkle with the crumbs, and drizzle with melted butter. (The casserole can be prepared up to 8 hours ahead to this point and refrigerated.)

5. Preheat the oven to 400 degrees. If the casserole has been made ahead, loosely cover with foil and bake for 15 minutes. Uncover and bake until the sauce is bubbly and the crumbs are pale golden, about 35 minutes total. If freshly prepared, bake, uncovered, for 25 to 30 minutes.

— *Note* —

Haddock is readily available in Maine and other parts of New England, but almost any mild, flaky white fish can substitute.

DOWN EAST CRAB CAKES

BRENDA HOPKINS, who lives on the island, is the best crab picker I know. Her boyfriend, Bill

Clark, is a lobster fisherman and she is his stern man. They catch the local peeky toe or rock crabs in their traps along with the lobsters. Instead of tossing them back overboard, like most lobstermen do, they bring the crabs home and Brenda steams them and then picks out the delicious meat. It's a painstaking process. Sometimes, if the crabs are small soft-shells, it might take several dozen crabs to produce a pound of meat. These crab cakes are one of the tastiest ways to prepare Brenda's crabmeat. *mg*

INGREDIENTS

1/2 CUP FRESH BREAD CRUMBS

1/4 CUP MAYONNAISE

1 TABLESPOON DRAINED CAPERS

2 TEASPOONS DIJON MUSTARD

2 TEASPOONS CHOPPED PARSLEY

2 TEASPOONS FRESH THYME OR 1 TEASPOON DRIED

1/2 TEASPOON WORCESTERSHIRE SAUCE

1/4 TEASPOON TABASCO SAUCE

2 LARGE EGGS, LIGHTLY BEATEN

12 OUNCES CRABMEAT, PICKED OVER TO REMOVE
ANY SHELL OR CARTILAGE

4 SCALLIONS, THINLY SLICED

2 TABLESPOONS (1/4 STICK) UNSALTED BUTTER

SERVES 4

1. In a large bowl, combine the bread crumbs, mayonnaise, capers, mustard, parsley, thyme, Worcestershire, Tabasco, and eggs. Stir in the crabmeat gently so as not to break up all the larger pieces. Stir in the scallions. Shape the mixture into eight cakes.

2. In one large or two smaller skillets, heat the butter. Cook the cakes over medium heat until golden brown outside and heated through within, about 4 minutes per side.

LINNY'S TOMALLEY & ROE ALL-GO LOBSTER STEW

THE BASIC LOBSTER STEW RECIPE—usually just lobster, cream, and butter—doesn't do it for me. I don't think it has much flavor. But if you use the tomalley and the roe (see Note), I am confident that just one taste and you'll never go back to throwing all this good stuff away. *lg*

INGREDIENTS

FOUR 1 1/2-POUND FEMALE LOBSTERS

1/4 POUND (1 STICK) UNSALTED BUTTER

1 TABLESPOON CHOPPED FRESH TARRAGON

6 CUPS MILK

2 CUPS HEAVY CREAM

1/3 CUP MADEIRA OR MEDIUM-DRY SHERRY

SALT

WHITE PEPPER

SERVES 8 AS A STARTER, 4 AS A MAIN COURSE

1. Steam or boil the lobster until the shells turn red, about 12 minutes. Drain, and when cool enough to handle, pick the meat from the lobsters, including the small pieces in the bodies. Reserve the tomalley (not more than 3 tablespoons) and any red roe that you get from the bodies and tails. Remove the black intestinal strip from the tails and cut the meat into bite-sized pieces.

2. In a large heavy pot, melt the butter. Add the tomalley and roe and cook over medium heat, crushing the roe with the back of a wooden spoon to break it up into small bits. Add the lobster meat and tarragon and cook for about 3 minutes. Add the milk, cream, and wine and bring to a simmer, stirring frequently. Season to taste with salt and white pepper. Set aside to cool until ready to serve. If not serving within a couple of hours, refrigerate. Heat gently before serving.

Note

Tomalley is the soft green material full of delicious flavor you find tucked away in the lobster bodies. Roe (also called coral) is brilliant red when cooked and less flavorful, but it adds pretty color to the stew.

LEMON SHRIMP PASTA SALAD

MY FRIEND MARY SERVED this shrimp and pasta salad to our bridge group for lunch not too long ago. I especially loved the lemony dressing, and she agreed to give me the recipe. When someone else asked Mary for the recipe she said, "Sorry. Now you need to wait for Martha's cookbook!" *mg*

CREAMY LEMON-GARLIC DRESSING

1 TEASPOON GRATED LEMON ZEST

3 TABLESPOONS LEMON JUICE

1 TEASPOON DIJON MUSTARD

1 TEASPOON WORCESTERSHIRE SAUCE

2 GARLIC CLOVES, CRUSHED THROUGH A PRESS OR MINCED

1/2 CUP LIGHT OLIVE OIL

1 TABLESPOON SOUR CREAM

1/2 TEASPOON SALT

1/4 TEASPOON FRESHLY GROUND BLACK PEPPER

SALAD

1/2 POUND ROTELLE (OR OTHER SIMILAR SHAPE) PASTA

1 CUP SNOW PEAS, HALVED DIAGONALLY IF LARGE

1 POUND COOKED MAINE SHRIMP, SHELLED AND DEVEINED

1/2 CUP THINLY SLICED SCALLIONS

2/3 CUP SLICED BLACK OLIVES

1 1/2 CUPS TOASTED CROUTONS

1/2 CUP GRATED PARMESAN CHEESE

6 CUPS TORN ROMAINE LEAVES

1 LEMON, THINLY SLICED, SLICES HALVED

SERVES 6

1. Make the dressing. In a small bowl, whisk together the lemon zest and juice, mustard, Worcestershire, and garlic. Whisk in the oil and sour cream. Season with salt and pepper.

2. Cook the pasta in a large pot of salted water until al dente, about 10 minutes. Add the snow peas to the pot for the last 30 seconds of cooking time. Drain into a colander, rinse with cold water, and drain again. Transfer to a large bowl. Add the shrimp, scallions, and olives and toss to combine. Add about 1/2 cup of the dressing or enough to coat and stir gently. Refrigerate for at least 1 hour to blend the flavors.

3. Before serving, add the croutons and cheese and toss gently. If the salad seems dry, add some or all of the remaining dressing. Spread a bed of lettuce onto one large platter or individual plates, spoon the salad over, garnish with lemon slices, and serve.

Note

It's easier to grate lemons before squeezing the juice. Cold lemons grate better than room-temperature lemons. It's worth investing in one of the new microplane graters, which are much, much sharper than the old box graters.

MAINE SHRIMP BISQUE

THIS BISQUE IS A FAMILY FAVORITE. During Maine shrimp season in the winter, Jim requests it often and I am happy to make it because I love this bisque, too. Sometimes, as a change of pace, I don't purée it so that it's really more like a shrimp and vegetable rice soup. *mg*

INGREDIENTS

3 TABLESPOONS UNSALTED BUTTER

1 1/2 POUNDS MAINE SHRIMP OR MEDIUM SHRIMP, SHELLED AND DEVEINED (SEE NOTE)

1 SMALL YELLOW ONION, CHOPPED

1 CELERY STALK, CHOPPED

1 CARROT, CHOPPED

2 TEASPOONS DRIED TARRAGON

1 1/2 TEASPOONS GRATED LEMON ZEST

1 CUP DRY WHITE WINE

1/4 CUP MADEIRA OR MEDIUM-DRY SHERRY

3 CUPS BOTTLED CLAM JUICE

1 CUP HEAVY CREAM

3 TABLESPOONS LONG-GRAIN WHITE RICE

2 TABLESPOONS TOMATO PASTE

SALT AND FRESHLY GROUND BLACK PEPPER

SERVES 8 AS A FIRST COURSE, 4 AS A MAIN COURSE

1. In a large pot, melt 2 tablespoons of the butter. Add the shrimp and sauté over medium heat until just cooked through, 3 to 5 minutes. Transfer the shrimp and juices to a bowl.

2. Add the remaining tablespoon of butter to the pan. Add the onion, celery, and carrot and cook until the vegetables begin to soften, about 5 minutes. Add the tarragon and lemon zest and cook 1 minute. Add the wine and sherry, raise the heat, and boil for 2 minutes. Add the clam juice, cream, rice, and tomato paste. Simmer, covered, until the rice is very tender, 20 to 25 minutes.

3. Set aside 8 shrimp for garnish. In a food processor, working in batches, purée the cooked shrimp with the liquid base until quite smooth. Season with salt and pepper to taste and adjust the amount of liquid if necessary. Cool and refrigerate for at least 8 hours or overnight.

4. When ready to serve, reheat gently and serve, garnished with the reserved shrimp.

Note

If you have shrimp shells, you can make a nice flavorful stock to use here in place of the bottled clam juice. Simply simmer the shells in 4 cups of water for about 15 minutes. Strain through a sieve, pressing the remaining liquid out of the solids. If you use frozen cooked Maine shrimp, sauté for only about 2 to 3 minutes.

MARTHA'S FAMOUS LOBSTER CASSEROLE

I ADMIT TO BEING PROUD OF "my daughter the author," and I was secretly tickled when she wrote about this casserole in her book *The Lobster Chronicles*, and even included an expanded version of the recipe. For that, I've even forgiven her for being unkind to my favorite pot. You'll have to read the book to find out what I mean! *mg*

INGREDIENTS

4 TABLESPOONS (1/2 STICK) UNSALTED BUTTER

4 TABLESPOONS ALL-PURPOSE FLOUR

2 CUPS LIGHT CREAM

3 TABLESPOONS MADEIRA OR MEDIUM-DRY SHERRY

1 EGG YOLK

1 TABLESPOON MINCED YELLOW ONION

1 TABLESPOON MINCED PARSLEY

1 TEASPOON SALT

1/2 TEASPOON FRESHLY GROUND BLACK PEPPER

1/2 TEASPOON CELERY SEED

DASH OF CAYENNE PEPPER

5 TO 6 CUPS COOKED LOBSTER MEAT, CUT INTO BITE-SIZED CHUNKS

1 1/2 CUPS FRESH BREAD CRUMBS

2 TABLESPOONS GRATED PARMESAN CHEESE

2 TABLESPOONS (1/4 STICK) UNSALTED BUTTER, MELTED

SERVES 6 TO 8

1. Butter a shallow 2-quart baking dish.

2. In a large saucepan or deep skillet, melt the butter. Add the flour and cook over medium heat, whisking, for 2 minutes. Whisk in the cream, bring to a simmer, and cook, whisking, until the sauce is smooth and thick, 3 to 4 minutes. In a small bowl, whisk together the sherry and egg yolk. Whisk a little of the hot sauce in to temper the egg yolk, then whisk the egg yolk mixture into the hot sauce. Add the onion, parsley, salt, pepper, celery seed, and cayenne, and stir in the lobster meat. Transfer to the prepared baking dish, sprinkle with the bread crumbs and Parmesan cheese, and drizzle with the melted butter. (The casserole can be prepared up to 8 hours ahead to this point and refrigerated.)

3. Preheat the oven to 400 degrees.

4. If cold, bake the casserole, loosely covered with foil for the first 15 minutes, until the sauce is bubbly and the crumbs are lightly browned, a total of about 35 minutes. If freshly prepared, bake, uncovered, for 20 to 25 minutes.

Note

You get about 1 cup of meat from a 1 1/4-pound lobster—a little less if it's a soft-shell.

POINT LOOKOUT LOBSTER SALAD

HERE'S A GREAT, SIMPLE LOBSTER SALAD that travels particularly well in summer because it contains no mayonnaise. We often pack up enough for lunch and go on an island picnic to Shark Point beach or to the swimming hole at Long Pond, which is a mile long. *mg*

INGREDIENTS

FOUR 1 1/2-POUND LOBSTERS

1 CUP FRESH OR FROZEN GREEN PEAS

1 CUP SLICED CELERY

2 TABLESPOONS MINCED FRESH BASIL LEAVES

1 TABLESPOON GRATED LEMON ZEST

6 TABLESPOONS FRESH LEMON JUICE

1/2 TEASPOON SALT, PLUS MORE TO TASTE

2/3 CUP OLIVE OIL

WHITE PEPPER

LEMON SLICES, FOR GARNISH

SERVES 4

1. Put the lobsters headfirst into a kettle of boiling salted water. Cover, let the water return to a boil, and cook for about 12 minutes, or until the lobster shells are bright red.

2. Transfer the lobsters to a cutting board. When cool enough to handle, remove the meat from the claws and tail and cut into 3/4-inch pieces. Transfer to a large bowl. (Or use 3 cups cold leftover lobster meat.)

3. Cook fresh peas in lightly salted water for 3 to 7 minutes (depending on size), or just until tender. Cook frozen peas for about 2 minutes, or until crisp-tender. Drain, rinse with cold water to cool, and pat dry on paper towels. Add to the lobster meat. Stir in the celery, basil, and lemon zest.

4. In a small bowl, whisk together the lemon juice and salt. Slowly add the oil in a steady stream, whisking the dressing until it is emulsified.

5. Pour enough dressing over the lobster mixture to coat the salad and toss gently. Season to taste with additional salt and white pepper.

6. Divide the salad among salad plates and garnish with lemon slices.

MADEIRA-SAUTÉED LOBSTER ON ANGEL HAIR PASTA

HERE'S A TYPICAL SCENARIO: I invite eight or so people for dinner in the morning. Not having a clue as to what I'm going to serve, I get busy checking out recipes in kitchen drawers, books, buffet drawers, bedroom nightstands, and so on. Quite often, I settle on Madeira-Sautéed Lobster with some sort of pasta. This means a call to the *Mattie Belle* on the VHF radio to ask Jim and Linda to bring back a dozen pound-and-a-halfers. When they arrive home from hauling, I put them to work boiling, cooling, and picking the lobster out of their shells. When our guests arrive, the Madeira lobster sauce is completed, so all that's left to do is cook the pasta and finish the dish. *mg*

INGREDIENTS

1/4 POUND (1 STICK) UNSALTED BUTTER

4 TABLESPOONS EXTRA-VIRGIN OLIVE OIL

1 MEDIUM YELLOW ONION, CHOPPED

4 GARLIC CLOVES, FINELY CHOPPED

4 CUPS BITE-SIZED CHUNKS COOKED LOBSTER MEAT

1/2 CUP MADEIRA OR MEDIUM-DRY SHERRY

SALT AND FRESHLY GROUND BLACK PEPPER

1 POUND ANGEL HAIR OR OTHER THIN-STRAND PASTA

SERVES 4

1. In a large wide skillet, heat the butter and oil. Add the onion and cook over medium heat until softened, about 5 minutes. Add the garlic and lobster meat and cook, stirring, for 3 to 4 minutes. Add 1/4 cup of the wine, bring to a boil, and cook for 1 minute to burn off the alcohol. Add the remaining 1/4 cup wine and season the sauce to taste with salt and pepper.

2. Meanwhile, cook the pasta in a large pot of boiling salted water until al dente, about 8 minutes. Drain.

3. Reheat the sauce if necessary, spoon over the pasta, toss if desired, and serve.

Note

You will need meat from about four 1 1/2-pound lobsters for this dish.

WICKED GOOD LOBSTER AND BLACK BEAN CHILI

WHEN MY FRIEND DICK TOLD ME about his new chili recipe, I had my doubts and told Patti, his wife, that I just couldn't imagine lobster and black beans together. Boy, was I wrong! Not only is this delicious, it's also beautiful to look at. *mg*

INGREDIENTS

1 POUND DRIED BLACK BEANS, RINSED

SALT

FOUR 1 1/2-POUND LOBSTERS

4 TABLESPOONS OLIVE OIL

1 YELLOW ONION, CHOPPED

3 GARLIC CLOVES, FINELY CHOPPED

3 JALAPEÑO PEPPERS, COARSELY CHOPPED

4 CUPS LOBSTER STOCK OR BOTTLED CLAM JUICE

ONE 28-OUNCE CAN CRUSHED TOMATOES

1 TABLESPOON DRIED OREGANO

2 TEASPOONS DRIED BASIL

1 TEASPOON DRIED THYME

1 BAY LEAF

8 TABLESPOONS (1 STICK) UNSALTED BUTTER

2 TABLESPOONS PAPRIKA, PREFERABLY HUNGARIAN SWEET PAPRIKA

2 TEASPOONS CHILI POWDER

1/3 CUP SNIPPED CHIVES

1/3 CUP CHOPPED CILANTRO

SERVES 8 TO 10

1. In a large pot, cover the beans with cold water, bring to a boil, and cook briskly for 5 minutes. Remove from the heat and let soak for 1 hour. Drain, rinse, and set aside.

2. Bring 2 inches of water to a boil in a large pot. Add 1 teaspoon of salt. Plunge the lobsters headfirst into the boiling water. Cover the pot, return to the boil, and cook until the lobsters turn red, about 10 minutes. Remove the lobsters with tongs, saving the cooking broth. When the lobsters are cool enough to handle, crack the shells and remove the meat, leaving the claw meat intact and cutting the tail meat into neat 2-inch pieces. Reserve. Return the shells to the cooking water and simmer for 20 minutes. Strain. Measure out 4 cups, making up any difference with water or clam juice. (Or, instead of making the lobster stock, use all bottled clam juice.)

3. In a large pot, heat the oil over medium heat. Add the onion, garlic, and peppers and cook, stirring often, until softened, about 5 minutes. Add the drained beans, the 4 cups seafood stock, tomatoes, oregano, basil, thyme, and bay leaf. Season with about 1/2 teaspoon salt. Bring to a boil, reduce the heat to very low, and cook, covered, until the beans are tender, 1 1/2 to 2 hours. Taste and season again with salt. (No salt may be necessary due to the saltiness of the stock or clam juice.)

4. In a large skillet, heat the butter. Sprinkle the reserved lobster meat with paprika and chili powder and sauté over medium heat until the spices are toasted and the lobster is heated through.

5. Ladle the beans into shallow soup bowls, arrange the lobster over the beans (stirring it in if you like), sprinkle with chives and cilantro, and serve.

Note

After working with jalapeños, wash your hands thoroughly. Most of the heat is in the ribs and seeds, so leave these in if you like more spiciness. You can also adjust the spiciness by adding more or less chili powder.

KEEPER'S HOUSE SCALLOPED SCALLOPS

THE KEEPER'S HOUSE, formerly the lighthouse keeper's dwelling on the west side of the island, is now an inn. Proudly run by Jeff and Judy Burke, they enjoy the unique history of the place, which has been the subject of many magazine and newspaper features. The Keeper's House is well known for its excellent dining room, and Judy was happy to share her wonderful scalloped scallops recipe with me. *mg*

INGREDIENTS

1 1/2 POUNDS SEA SCALLOPS, CUT IN HALF IF VERY LARGE

1/2 CUP DRY WHITE WINE

1 CUP FRESH BREAD CRUMBS

3 TABLESPOONS PARMESAN CHEESE

1 TABLESPOON MINCED GARLIC

2 TABLESPOONS SNIPPED CHIVES

SALT AND WHITE PEPPER TO TASTE

4 TABLESPOONS (1/2 STICK) UNSALTED BUTTER

2 TABLESPOONS CHOPPED PARSLEY

2 TABLESPOONS LEMON JUICE

LEMON WEDGES, FOR GARNISH

SERVES 4

1. Butter a shallow baking dish or four individual ramekins.

2. Place the scallops in the bottom of the dish(es) and drizzle the white wine over.

3. In a bowl, toss the bread crumbs with the Parmesan cheese, garlic, chives, and salt and pepper. Sprinkle over the scallops.

4. Melt the butter and stir in the parsley and lemon juice. Drizzle over the crumbs. (The casserole(s) can be made ahead and refrigerated for up to 4 hours.)

5. Preheat the oven to 400 degrees.

6. Bake the casserole(s), uncovered, until the scallops are opaque and the crumbs are lightly browned, 15 to 20 minutes if made fresh, about 30 minutes if refrigerated. Garnish with lemon wedges and serve.

GRILLED MARINATED SCALLOPS WITH GINGER AND SESAME

A FRIEND WHO SPENDS THE WINTER MONTHS dragging for scallops showed up at my door one evening bearing a gift of two gallons of freshly shucked scallops. (This may have been due to the fact that he had overimbibed at a party on a previous night, passed out in the middle of my kitchen floor, and had to be carried home. The gift was appreciated and he was forgiven.) The scallops were gorgeous! Although scallops do freeze well, nothing compares to those straight out of the shell. I tried to consume as many scallops as I could while they were fresh. Luckily, I also love them marinated and grilled. They only way to hurt them is to dry them out by overcooking. Like most seafood, to err on the side of undercooked is divine! *lg*

INGREDIENTS

1/2 CUP PINEAPPLE JUICE

1/2 CUP SOY SAUCE

1 TABLESPOON GRATED FRESH GINGER

ZEST AND JUICE OF 1 LIME

24 LARGE SEA SCALLOPS

3 TABLESPOONS SESAME SEEDS

LIME WEDGES, FOR GARNISH

SERVES 4

1. In a shallow dish, combine the pineapple juice, soy sauce, ginger, lime zest, and lime juice. Add the scallops, turn to coat, and set aside for 30 to 40 minutes.
2. Build a hot charcoal fire or preheat a gas grill. Toast the sesame seeds in a small skillet over medium heat until they turn one shade darker, about 4 minutes.
3. Thread the scallops on four metal skewers, placing them so that the flat surfaces are exposed. Grill, turning once, until the scallops are lightly browned and no longer translucent, about 2 to 3 minutes per side. Sprinkle with sesame seeds, garnish with lime wedges, and serve.

MUSSELS LINGUINE

THIS IS A GREAT-TASTING MUSSEL DISH. I make it often, either with the wild mussels that live on our rocks and ledges or with Dave Hiltz's rope-grown mussels from his float in the harbor. It's also a nice recipe to know about if you happen to have cooked mussels left over from a mussel feast. *mg*

INGREDIENTS

3 POUNDS MUSSELS, SCRUBBED

1/2 CUP DRY WHITE WINE

1/2 CUP OLIVE OIL

3 GARLIC CLOVES, SLICED THIN

HALF A DRIED RED CHILI PEPPER, CRUMBLED, OR 1/2 TEASPOON DRIED RED PEPPER FLAKES

3 TABLESPOONS CHOPPED PARSLEY

SALT AND FRESHLY GROUND BLACK PEPPER

1 POUND LINGUINE

SERVES 4

1. Combine the mussels and wine in a large pot. Cover, bring to a boil, and steam until the mussels open, 4 to 10 minutes, depending on size. Use a slotted spoon to remove the mussels to a bowl, discarding any that do not open. When cool enough to handle, shell the mussels and reserve the meat. (If you like, reserve some mussels in the shells for garnish.) Reserve the cooking liquid, letting any sediment settle to the bottom of the pot.

2. In a medium-large skillet, heat the oil. Add the garlic and chili pepper and cook over medium heat until the garlic is pale gold, about 2 minutes. Add the mussels, reserved cooking liquid (leaving any sediment behind), and 2 tablespoons of the parsley. Simmer, uncovered, for 5 minutes. Season with salt and pepper to taste.

3. Cook the pasta in a large pot of rapidly boiling salted water until al dente, about 10 minutes. Drain, reserving about a cup of the cooking water. Transfer to a large serving bowl, spoon half the sauce over, and toss. Spoon the remaining sauce over the pasta, adding a bit of the reserved cooking water if it seems dry. Garnish with the reserved mussels in shells if desired, sprinkle with the remaining tablespoon of parsley, and serve.

PEMAQUID OYSTER STEW
WITH GUINNESS AND VIDALIA ONIONS

ONE SNOWY WINTER EVENING I wandered into an Irish pub in Portland, Maine, where the special of the evening was Oysters Guinness, made with Maine oysters from Pemaquid. I ordered a bowl and was tempted to lick the inside of the crockery—it was that good. I'm shy about asking chefs for recipes and thought I'd try to reproduce the stew on my own. I haven't quite perfected it yet, but this is pretty darned close! *lg*

INGREDIENTS

4 TABLESPOONS (1/2 STICK) UNSALTED BUTTER

1 LARGE VIDALIA ONION, SLICED

1 CUP EVAPORATED MILK

1 CUP HEAVY CREAM

2 CUPS MILK

1 CUP GUINNESS STOUT OR OTHER DARK BEER

1 PINT SHUCKED OYSTERS WITH LIQUOR

1 TABLESPOON CHOPPED FRESH TARRAGON

SALT AND WHITE PEPPER

SERVES 4 AS A FIRST COURSE

1. In a deep heavy saucepan, melt the butter. Add the onion and cook over medium heat until softened, about 8 minutes. Add the evaporated milk, cream, milk, and stout. Cook over medium heat, stirring frequently, until steam begins to rise, about 5 minutes. Do not boil. Add the oysters and their liquor and simmer on low heat until their edges begin to curl, 3 to 4 minutes. Add the tarragon and season to taste with salt and white pepper. Cool and refrigerate for at least 6 hours or overnight. (This allows the flavors to develop.)
2. When ready to serve, reheat the stew over very low heat, being careful not to boil.

CUNDY'S HARBOR SHRIMP CASSEROLES

EVERY WINTER JIM AND I look forward to the Maine shrimp season, which is never long enough to suit us. We especially love going to Holbrook's Dock in Cundy's Harbor, Maine, to sample that day's catch. They cook the tiny fresh shrimp (with heads on) for the workers, boiling them up in fifty-five-gallon drums in the fish house—and then offer tastes to the customers as complimentary snacks. After eating all we can hold—and catching up on all the local news of the day—we usually buy ten pounds to take home and cook, and this is one of my tried-and-true Maine shrimp recipes. These days you can usually buy the small shrimp frozen here in New England, but medium shrimp are a fine substitute. *mg*

INGREDIENTS

2 TABLESPOONS (1/4 STICK) UNSALTED BUTTER

1/2 POUND MUSHROOMS, SLICED

1/4 CUP CHOPPED YELLOW ONION

ONE 14 1/2-OUNCE CAN DICED TOMATOES

3 TABLESPOONS ALL-PURPOSE FLOUR

1/2 CUP LIGHT CREAM

1/4 CUP MEDIUM-DRY SHERRY

1/4 TEASPOON PAPRIKA

DASH OF ANGOSTURA BITTERS

DASH OF TABASCO SAUCE

2 POUNDS SHELLED AND DEVEINED MAINE SHRIMP, RAW OR COOKED

2 TABLESPOONS CHOPPED PARSLEY

SALT AND FRESHLY GROUND BLACK PEPPER

1 CUP FRESH BREAD CRUMBS

2 TABLESPOONS (1/4 STICK) UNSALTED BUTTER, MELTED

SERVES 6

1. Butter six individual ramekins or one shallow 2-quart baking dish.

2. In a very large skillet, heat the butter. Add the mushrooms and onion and cook over medium-high heat, stirring frequently, until the mushroom liquid begins to evaporate, about 5 minutes. Add the tomatoes and simmer, uncovered, over medium heat for 10 minutes.

3. In a small bowl, whisk the flour and cream together. Pour the cream mixture into the skillet, whisking constantly, and cook for 2 minutes. Add the sherry, paprika, bitters, and Tabasco and simmer for 2 minutes. The sauce should be quite thick at this point because the shrimp will dilute it.

4. Add the shrimp to the sauce. If the shrimp are raw, cook for about 5 minutes, until the shrimp turn pink. If cooked, simmer for about 2 minutes to heat through. Stir in the parsley and season to taste with salt and pepper. Transfer to the prepared dish(es). Sprinkle with the bread crumbs and drizzle with melted butter. (The casserole(s) can be made up to a day ahead and refrigerated.)

5. Preheat the oven to 375 degrees.

6. If casseroles have been refrigerated, bake, uncovered, for about 40 minutes, or until heated through and the crumbs are lightly browned. If at room temperature, bake for about 30 minutes.

SPECIAL SCALLOPED OYSTERS

THIS RICH AND ELEGANT CASSEROLE is a hit with everybody—even oyster haters. I usually use the pasteurized oysters that are now pretty easy to find in supermarket seafood departments. *mg*

INGREDIENTS

3 TABLESPOONS UNSALTED BUTTER

3 TABLESPOONS ALL-PURPOSE FLOUR

1/2 CUP WHIPPING CREAM

1/2 CUP CHICKEN STOCK

1/2 CUP DRY WHITE WINE

1 TABLESPOON LEMON JUICE

SALT AND FRESHLY GROUND BLACK PEPPER

PINCH OF GRATED NUTMEG

1 PINT OYSTERS

2 CUPS PACKAGED UNSEASONED CROUTONS, LIGHTLY CRUSHED

1/4 CUP GRATED PARMESAN CHEESE

PAPRIKA

SERVES 4

1. Butter a 1 1/2-quart baking dish. Preheat the oven to 425 degrees.

2. In a heavy saucepan, melt the butter. Add the flour and cook over medium heat, whisking, for 2 minutes. Whisk in the cream and stock, bring to a boil, and cook, whisking, for 2 minutes. Add the wine and lemon juice and season to taste with salt, pepper, and nutmeg.

3. Place half the oysters in the prepared baking dish; sprinkle with half the croutons and half the sauce. Repeat the layers and sprinkle cheese over the top. Dust with paprika.

4. Bake until the sauce is bubbly and the top is lightly browned, 20 to 30 minutes.

ISLAND LOBSTER ROLLS

DURING THE SUMMER MONTHS, lobster rolls are by far the most popular lunch item on the Maine coast. When I open the refrigerator and see that we have some lobster left over from dinner the night before, lobster rolls are most definitely on the menu for our lunch! Please save room on the plates for potato chips. *mg*

INGREDIENTS

3 CUPS DICED LOBSTER MEAT

1/4 CUP BOTTLED OR HOMEMADE VINAIGRETTE DRESSING (PAGE 176)

1/2 CUP FINELY DICED CELERY

1/2 CUP MAYONNAISE, OR TO TASTE

2 TABLESPOONS (1/4 STICK) UNSALTED BUTTER

4 TOP-SPLIT FRANKFURTER ROLLS

SERVES 4

1. In a bowl, toss the lobster meat with the dressing. Refrigerate for at least 2 hours.
2. Drain the lobster and discard the dressing. Add the celery and mayonnaise and stir to combine, adding more mayonnaise if needed to moisten well.
3. Melt the butter on a cast-iron griddle or in a large frying pan. Place the rolls in the butter, cut sides down, and toast over medium heat, turning once, until browned on both edges. Fill with lobster salad and serve.

CHAPTER 3

FISH THAT SWIM IN THE SEA

FRESH CODFISH CAKES WITH CHILI MAYO

THIS RECIPE CAN BE MADE with nearly any type of fish. I've used salmon, haddock, pollock, and hake, but I like cod best. The cakes can be shaped and refrigerated for up to a couple of days before frying, and the chili mayo can also be prepared ahead. It's a nice alternative to traditional tartar sauce. *lg*

CHILI MAYO

1/2 CUP MAYONNAISE

1/2 CUP PLAIN FAT-FREE YOGURT

1 TABLESPOON CHILI POWDER, OR TO TASTE

1 TEASPOON LEMON JUICE

1 TO 2 TEASPOONS JALAPEÑO SALSA (OPTIONAL)

FISH CAKES

4 BACON STRIPS

1 1/2 POUNDS (ABOUT 6 MEDIUM) ALL-PURPOSE POTATOES

SALT

1 POUND FRESH COD

1 LARGE ONION, CHOPPED

2 LARGE EGGS, LIGHTLY BEATEN

2 TABLESPOONS CHOPPED FRESH TARRAGON

FRESHLY GROUND BLACK PEPPER

1/2 CUP ALL-PURPOSE FLOUR

2 TABLESPOONS UNSALTED BUTTER

2 TABLESPOONS LIGHT OLIVE OIL

SERVES 4

1. For the chili mayo, whisk all the ingredients together in a small bowl and refrigerate until ready to serve.

2. For the fish cakes, cook the bacon in a skillet over medium heat until crisp, 10 to 12 minutes. Drain on paper towels, leaving the drippings in the pan.

3. Peel the potatoes and cut into 1/2-inch cubes. Cook in boiling salted water until soft, about 10 minutes. Drain and transfer to a large bowl.

4. Bring a skillet of lightly salted water to a boil. Add the cod and poach in simmering water until the fish flakes easily with a fork, 5 to 8 minutes. Drain and break or chop into small chunks and add to the potatoes.

5. Cook the onion over medium heat in the bacon drippings until slightly softened, about 3 minutes. Add to the potato mixture. Crumble the bacon and add it to the bowl along with the eggs and the tarragon. Work the mixture together with your hands until well blended. Season with black pepper and additional salt to taste. Shape into 8 cakes about 1/2 inch thick. Spread the flour onto a plate; dredge the cakes in the flour.

6. Heat the butter and oil in one very large or two smaller frying pans. Cook the fish cakes over medium to medium-high heat, turning once, until browned and slightly crisp on both sides and heated through inside, about 10 minutes. Pass the chili mayo for spooning on top.

Note

This is a great way to use leftover fish.

GULF OF MAINE HADDOCK CASSEROLE

YOU WOULDN'T BELIEVE HOW GOOD THIS SIMPLE CASSEROLE IS! It's one of the specialties of Mary Ann, a longtime member of our gourmet group, who has served it to the group on many an occasion. Mary Ann said recently, "Not again. Let's give it a rest." But we all like it so much that I'm not sure we'll let her quit making it. *mg*

INGREDIENTS

1 1/2 POUNDS HADDOCK FILLETS

1 SLEEVE (36) RITZ CRACKERS, CRUSHED (ABOUT 1 1/3 CUPS)

2 CUPS SHREDDED CHEDDAR CHEESE

ONE 10 3/4-OUNCE CAN CREAM OF SHRIMP SOUP

1/2 CUP MILK

PAPRIKA

SERVES 4

1. Butter a 2-quart shallow baking dish. Preheat the oven to 350 degrees.
2. Cut the fish into 3/4-inch pieces and place half in the prepared dish. Sprinkle with half the cracker crumbs and half the cheese. Repeat, layering the fish and crumbs. Whisk the soup with the milk, pour over the top, and sprinkle with the rest of the cheese.
3. Bake until the fish is cooked through, the sauce is bubbly, and the top is lightly browned, about 35 minutes. Sprinkle with paprika and serve.

Note

You can also use leftover fish for this dish.

Bread Bags

I RECENTLY RECEIVED the following e-mail from my older sister, Rhonda:

Hi Linny,

Hey, do you remember wearing plastic bread bags as waterproof boot liners when we were kids? Isn't that the funniest thing? "Hey Mom! There are two slices of bread left. Hurry up and make me a sandwich! I need to go out in the snow!" Remember searching frantically for rubber bands to hold them up? Remember what your calves looked like when you took them off?

I did remember this with a smile, and also recalled our never disposing of empty egg cartons, although I can't think of a single use for them now. Yankee ingenuity is something we staunch New Englanders take pride in. We understand the multi-usefulness of any item and are therefore hesitant to throw things away. Most items are hoarded just for their potential. Our barns, garages, and basements are literal warehouses. Our yards are stockpiles of mothballed boats, lawn tractors, cars, refrigerators, and yes, even furniture that may be viewed by those less thrifty as junk. But we know this junk as inventory, and never make a trip to the hardware or auto-parts store for something that could be scavenged from the rusted heap behind the woodpile. Hubcaps adorn tarpaper, and old tires are cut and painted into decorative planters. We gleefully return from the town dump carrying more than we left with. Where, other than New England, are flea markets and yard sales so well attended? Who, other than a native New Englander, would spend three dollars on something advertised as "box and contents"?

This propensity toward frugality leaks into our eating habits. Our composts don't see much in the way of table scraps. We eat hash and "refrigerator soup." Others may marvel at the technology

of Shake-and-Bake, Slice-and-Bake, and Pop-n-Fresh, while we New Englanders have perfected Scrape-and-Serve. Orr's Island native Walter Leeman professes, "God's greatest gift to mankind is the sow hake" (a very large, lesser-known fish), and he boasts that he can stretch one fish to feed himself four consecutive dinners. "I fry it the first night, corn it the second, make hash the third, and my favorite fish cakes are last." I have opened Walter's refrigerator on many occasions over the past twenty years and have never seen it void of hake in its various stages of the four-day meal plan. Any uncooked fillets are stored in—you guessed it—bread bags! *lg*

GRILLED HALIBUT WITH BASIL BUTTER

WE DO A LOT OF GRILLING in the summer months, especially of fish. Halibut is great cooked on  the grill, but it can be dry if overcooked, so be careful! We make this basil butter when we get hold of a nice bunch of that fragrant summer herb. *lg*

INGREDIENTS

1/4 CUP LIGHTLY PACKED BASIL LEAVES, PLUS SPRIGS FOR GARNISH

2 TABLESPOONS PARSLEY SPRIGS

1 SCALLION, CUT INTO 1-INCH LENGTHS

4 TABLESPOONS (1/2 STICK) UNSALTED BUTTER, SOFTENED

2 TEASPOONS LEMON JUICE

1/8 TEASPOON FRESHLY GROUND BLACK PEPPER

2 TABLESPOONS GRATED PARMESAN CHEESE

SIX 6-OUNCE HALIBUT STEAKS OR FILLETS, CUT ABOUT 1 INCH THICK

SLICED TOMATOES, FOR GARNISH

SERVES 6

1. In a food processor fitted with a metal blade, pulse the basil, parsley, and scallion until coarsely chopped. Add butter, lemon juice, and pepper and process until combined. Remove and reserve about one-quarter of the mixture for basting the fish. Add cheese to the remainder and process until smooth.

2. Build a medium-hot charcoal fire or preheat a gas grill. Spread the reserved basil butter over both sides of the fish. Place the fish in an oiled fish basket or directly on well-oiled grill grids. Cover with the grill lid and cook, turning once, until the fish is no longer translucent in the center. Check after 5 minutes and continue to cook for a few minutes more if needed.

3. Transfer to warm plates or a platter, top with the remaining basil butter, garnish with tomatoes and basil sprigs, and serve.

Note

A fish basket is handy for cooking any fish on a grill, especially the more delicate varieties that tend to fall apart during cooking. Halibut is somewhere in the middle—that is, it's fairly sturdy, but it doesn't hold together as well as swordfish or tuna.

HADDOCK CHOWDER

MAINERS ARE REALLY PARTIAL to their local fresh haddock. It's their fish of choice for many things—fried fish sandwiches, fish and chips, and sautéed fish—but I think haddock is especially well suited to chowder. It has great flavor and the perfect texture because it easily breaks up into nice large chunks in the soup. If you possibly can, try to make the chowder a day ahead. It greatly improves if allowed to age or cure overnight in the refrigerator. *mg*

INGREDIENTS

3 POUNDS HADDOCK

6 BACON SLICES, ROUGHLY DICED

3 ONIONS, SLICED

2 TABLESPOONS ALL-PURPOSE FLOUR

3 CUPS BOTTLED CLAM JUICE

5 MEDIUM ALL-PURPOSE POTATOES, SCRUBBED AND CUBED

2 CUPS MILK

TWO 12-OUNCE CANS EVAPORATED MILK

1 TABLESPOON UNSALTED BUTTER

4 SHAKES PAPRIKA

1/4 TEASPOON MACE

1 TABLESPOON CHOPPED FLAT-LEAF PARSLEY

SERVES 6

1. In a large pot, bring water or a mixture of water and clam juice or fish stock to a simmer over medium heat. Add the haddock and poach the fish for 10 to 12 minutes, or until the fish is firm but not flaking. Lift the fish from the poaching liquid and set aside until cool enough to handle. Reserve the poaching liquid.

2. In a stockpot set over medium heat, fry the bacon until crisp and brown, about 10 minutes. Remove the bacon with a slotted spoon and drain on paper towels, leaving the fat in the pot.

3. Add the onion slices to the bacon fat and cook over medium-high heat for about 5 minutes, or until softened. Sprinkle with flour and cook, stirring, for 2 minutes. Add the clam juice and potatoes. Bring to a boil, reduce the heat to a simmer, and cook for 10 to 15 minutes, or until the potatoes are fork-tender.

4. Meanwhile, combine the milk and evaporated milk in a saucepan and heat over medium heat until hot. Do not boil.

5. Break up the cooked haddock and add to the pot. Add the heated milk, butter, and reserved bacon and season with the paprika and mace. If more liquid is needed, add some reserved poaching liquid. If time allows, cool the chowder, cover, and refrigerate overnight.

6. Reheat the chowder gently until hot and serve, garnished with parsley.

GRILLED SALMON WITH FRESH BLUEBERRY CORN SALSA

I LOVE FRESH SALSA with grilled fish and this is an unusual (and very colorful) salsa, made with blueberries and corn. I like to make it at the height of summer when both are in season. *lg*

INGREDIENTS

ONE 3-POUND FRESH SALMON FILLET

1 TABLESPOON GROUND CUMIN

SALT AND FRESHLY GROUND BLACK PEPPER

4 EARS SWEET CORN

4 MEDIUM TOMATOES, DICED

2 SMALL FIRM BUT RIPE AVOCADOS, PEELED AND DICED

1 SMALL GREEN BELL PEPPER, DICED

1 SMALL ORANGE BELL PEPPER, DICED

1 SMALL BUNCH CILANTRO, CHOPPED

JUICE OF 2 LIMES

2 TABLESPOONS OLIVE OIL

1 TABLESPOON RED WINE VINEGAR

2 CUPS BLUEBERRIES, PREFERABLY WILD MAINE BERRIES

SERVES 6

1. Sprinkle the salmon with the cumin and salt and pepper to taste. Refrigerate until ready to cook.

2. Cook the corn in boiling water about 5 minutes, cool, then cut the kernels from the cob. Combine in a bowl with the tomatoes, avocados, bell peppers, cilantro, lime juice, oil, and vinegar. Refrigerate until ready to serve.

3. Build a hot charcoal fire or preheat a gas grill. Cook the salmon, turning once, until it is charred—almost blackened—on the outside and has reached the desired degree of doneness within. I like it still quite juicy, bordering on rare.

4. Add the blueberries to the salsa, stirring them in gently so as to avoid mushing them. Season with salt and pepper to taste. Serve the salmon with the salsa spooned over.

— *Note* —

In a pinch, you could use 1 cup of thawed frozen corn kernels instead of the fresh corn.

GRILLED SWORDFISH WITH DOUBLE MUSTARD SAUCE

THE FLAVOR OF MUSTARD SEEMS to go great with swordfish. This recipe couldn't be simpler, but I receive rave reviews from guests every time! *mg*

INGREDIENTS

FOUR 8-OUNCE SWORDFISH STEAKS, ABOUT 1 1/2 INCHES THICK

2 TABLESPOONS OLIVE OIL

1/4 CUP FRESH LEMON JUICE

3 TABLESPOONS DIJON MUSTARD

6 TABLESPOONS (3/4 STICK) UNSALTED BUTTER

SERVES 4

1. Build a hot charcoal fire or preheat a gas grill. Pat the fish dry and brush both sides with the oil and 2 tablespoons of lemon juice. Spread one side with 2 tablespoons of the mustard and dot with 2 tablespoons of the butter. Grill, mustard side up, until the fish is just opaque, 10 to 15 minutes. Do not turn.

2. Meanwhile, in a small saucepan, melt the remaining 4 tablespoons butter. Add the remaining 2 tablespoons lemon juice and remaining tablespoon mustard and whisk until smooth.

3. Arrange the fish, mustard side down, on a platter, pour the sauce over, and serve.

GRILLED SWORDFISH
WITH TOMATO AND SWEET PEPPER SALSA

HERE'S ANOTHER TERRIFIC SALSA, which we make when someone gives us a big bag of tomatoes and peppers from their garden. It's delicious on fish, but also on just about everything else—chicken, scrambled eggs—or just used as a dip. *mg*

INGREDIENTS

2 RIPE TOMATOES, SEEDED AND CHOPPED

1/3 CUP DICED GREEN PEPPER

1/3 CUP DICED YELLOW PEPPER

1/3 CUP DICED RED ONION

2 TABLESPOONS, PLUS 2 TEASPOONS OLIVE OIL

2 TABLESPOONS FRESH LIME JUICE

2 TABLESPOONS RED WINE VINEGAR

1 LARGE GARLIC CLOVE, CRUSHED THROUGH A PRESS OR MINCED

1 TABLESPOON CHOPPED FRESH BASIL

1 TEASPOON CHOPPED FRESH THYME

SALT AND FRESHLY GROUND BLACK PEPPER

FOUR 6-OUNCE SWORDFISH STEAKS, ABOUT 1 1/2 INCHES THICK

SERVES 4

1. In a large bowl, combine the tomatoes, green pepper, yellow pepper, red onion, 2 tablespoons oil, lime juice, vinegar, garlic, basil, and thyme. Season with salt and pepper to taste. The salsa can be made up to 3 hours ahead.

2. Build a hot charcoal fire or preheat a gas grill. Brush the fish with the remaining 2 teaspoons of oil and season with salt and pepper. Grill, turning once, until nicely charred and the fish is just cooked through, about 5 minutes per side.

3. Spoon the salsa over the fish and serve.

— *Note* —

Swordfish steaks are often quite large, so simply cut the large piece of fish into serving-sized pieces.

CORNED HAKE

THIS IS A VERY OLD RECIPE that comes from the days when fish was salted (or corned) to preserve it. With the exception of deep-frying, it's perhaps the most unhealthy way to prepare fish. Between the salt and the pork scraps, I would not recommend a steady diet of corned hake, but as an occasional treat it's worth it. The first time I tasted corned hake was several years ago when the captain of a commercial fishing boat fixed it as a special treat for his crew. (This was a memorable occasion itself, because it's rare that a captain actually cooks.) He started with a fresh hake, which he buried in a pound of table salt for a day or so. The corned fish then gets "freshened" in several changes of water to remove most of the excess salt, then cooked. If you can't get your hands on a hake, any salt fish, such as salt cod, will do just fine. *lg*

INGREDIENTS

2 POUNDS HEAVILY SALTED HAKE FILLETS

2 MEDIUM ONIONS, CHOPPED COARSE

1 CUP APPLE CIDER VINEGAR OR OTHER VINEGAR (ANYTHING BUT BALSAMIC)

3/4 CUP FINELY DICED SALT PORK OR FATBACK

3 POUNDS POTATOES, PEELED AND CUT INTO 2-INCH CHUNKS

UNSALTED BUTTER

FRESHLY GROUND BLACK PEPPER

SERVES 6

1. Soak the corned hake in water to cover overnight to freshen, changing the water three or four times.

2. In a small bowl, combine the onions and vinegar. Set aside at room temperature.

3. Cook the salt pork in a frying pan over medium heat until it renders its fat and browns, about 10 minutes. Leave in the pan and reheat gently when ready to serve.

4. In another skillet, cover the fish with water, bring to a boil, reduce to a simmer, and cook gently until it flakes, about 15 minutes. Drain when ready to serve.

5. Cook the potatoes in boiling salted water until tender, about 15 minutes.

6. When ready to serve, mash a serving of potato on your plate with a fork and top with butter as you like. Place some fish on top of the potato. Top the fish with a few spoonfuls of pork bits and grease. Top the whole works with the vinegared onions and plenty of black pepper.

LINNY'S SPICY PAN-FRIED HORSE MACKEREL FINGERS WITH CITRUS TARTAR SAUCE

WHEN THE MACKEREL ARE RUNNING, any idiot can catch them. Unfortunately, as far as I'm concerned, there's not much you can do with a mackerel to make it less than nasty. But for those mackerel lovers out there, here's a way to cook it so it can really be enjoyed. You'll need four nice big fat mackerel ("horse" mackerel, as opposed to the smaller fish called "tinker" mackerel) that are big enough to be filleted. *lg*

CITRUS TARTAR SAUCE

1/2 CUP MAYONNAISE

1/2 CUP SOUR CREAM

ZEST AND JUICE OF 1 LIME

3 TABLESPOONS SWEET PICKLE RELISH

3 TABLESPOONS MINCED RED ONION

2 GARLIC CLOVES, RUN THROUGH A PRESS

DASH OF WORCESTERSHIRE SAUCE

MACKEREL

4 LARGE FRESH MACKEREL (ABOUT 1 TO 1 1/4 POUNDS EACH)

1/2 CUP ALL-PURPOSE FLOUR

1/2 CUP SEAFOOD SEASONING, SUCH AS OLD BAY

2 TABLESPOONS UNSALTED BUTTER

2 TABLESPOONS VEGETABLE OIL

SERVES 4

1. For the sauce, whisk all the ingredients together in a small bowl and refrigerate until ready to serve.
2. Skin the mackerel, cut the fillets off the bones, and cut each piece in half the long way. This should result in 16 pieces of fish.
3. On a plate, combine the flour and seafood seasoning and dredge the mackerel fingers in the seasoned flour.
4. Heat the butter and oil in one very large or two smaller skillets. Fry the fish over medium to medium-high heat until browned and crisp, about 6 minutes. Drain on paper towels and serve with the Citrus Tartar Sauce.

PAN-FRIED HALIBUT WITH FRESH TOMATO SAUCE

IN **LATE SPRING, OUR FRIENDS LINCOLN TULLY, ED WHITE,** and a couple of other fishermen set out halibut lines at daybreak several miles offshore from Isle au Haut. We all wait with great anticipation for them to return home just before dark. If they have had luck, we will have fresh halibut for dinner that night— either grilled or prepared in this sauce, which is inspired by a Portuguese dish called escabeche. *mg*

INGREDIENTS

2 POUNDS HALIBUT STEAKS

SALT

1/2 CUP ALL-PURPOSE FLOUR

1/2 CUP OLIVE OIL, PLUS ADDITIONAL IF NECESSARY

4 GARLIC CLOVES, MINCED OR CRUSHED IN A PRESS

3 LARGE TOMATOES, SEEDED AND COARSELY CHOPPED

6 TABLESPOONS RED WINE VINEGAR

1 TABLESPOON CHOPPED FRESH ROSEMARY OR
1 TABLESPOON CRUMBLED DRIED ROSEMARY

3 BAY LEAVES, PLUS ADDITIONAL FOR GARNISH

FRESHLY GROUND BLACK PEPPER

SERVES 4 TO 6

1. Remove any skin and bones from the halibut and cut into strips about 1/2 inch wide. Sprinkle the fish with salt and dredge in the flour, shaking off the excess. Heat 1/4 cup of the oil in a large heavy skillet over medium heat. When the oil is hot, add the fish and cook, turning with tongs, until nicely brown, 3 to 4 minutes. Remove and drain on paper towels. Repeat with a second batch of fish, adding more oil if needed.

2. Add enough oil to the skillet to measure 1/4 cup. Add the garlic and cook over medium heat for 30 seconds. Add the tomatoes, vinegar, rosemary, and bay leaves. Bring to a boil, reduce the heat to medium-low, and cook, uncovered, until the sauce thickens, about 15 minutes. Season to taste with pepper.

3. Arrange the fish on a platter and pour the sauce over. Cool and serve at room temperature or refrigerate for up to 24 hours. Return to room temperature before serving. Garnish with bay leaves.

SALMON CAKES WITH PEA AND MINT SAUCE

SALMON, PEAS, AND MINT are all available (theoretically) at about the same time in early summer in New England, so they were often served in combination at traditional Independence Day dinners. In fact, on the dairy farm in Winslow where I grew up, we ate broiled salmon and fresh peas in cream sauce every Fourth of July. This recipe is an elegant way to put these same ingredients together. You can get most of the work done ahead of time and finish it shortly before serving. *mg*

SALMON CAKES

1 1/2 POUNDS SKINLESS, BONELESS SALMON

6 SCALLIONS, FINELY CHOPPED

2 TABLESPOONS MINCED FRESH GINGER

1 LARGE EGG, LIGHTLY BEATEN

1 TABLESPOON LEMON JUICE

1 TEASPOON SOY SAUCE

1/2 TEASPOON SALT

1/4 TEASPOON FRESHLY GROUND BLACK PEPPER

1/4 CUP LIGHT OLIVE OIL OR VEGETABLE OIL

PEA AND MINT SAUCE

1 TABLESPOON UNSALTED BUTTER

1 TABLESPOON MINCED SHALLOTS

1/2 CUP DRY WHITE WINE

1 CUP HEAVY CREAM

1 1/4 CUPS FRESH OR FROZEN PEAS, COARSELY CHOPPED (SEE NOTE)

1 TEASPOON LEMON JUICE

2 TABLESPOONS CHOPPED FRESH MINT

SALT AND FRESHLY GROUND BLACK PEPPER

SERVES 4 TO 6

1. Place the salmon on a baking sheet and place in the freezer until partially frozen. Using a large chef's knife, chop the salmon medium-fine. Combine in a large bowl with the scallions, ginger, egg, lemon juice, soy sauce, salt, and pepper and mix gently but thoroughly to blend. Refrigerate until ready to make the cakes.

2. For the sauce, melt the butter in a large saucepan. Add the shallots and cook over medium heat for 1 minute. Add the wine, bring to a boil, and cook briskly until reduced by about half, about 2 minutes. Add the cream and simmer over medium heat until slightly reduced and thickened, about 4 minutes. Add the peas and simmer for about 5 minutes, until the peas are tender and the sauce is thick enough to heavily coat the back of a spoon. (The sauce can be made ahead and refrigerated or set aside at cool room temperature for up to several hours. Reheat gently before finishing.) Stir in the lemon juice and mint and season with salt and pepper.

3. To cook the salmon cakes, heat the oil in two large skillets. Using a 1/4-cup measure, spoon the salmon mixture into the skillets to make 12 cakes. Cook over medium heat until browned on the

bottom, about 3 minutes. Turn carefully with a spatula, cover the pans, and cook until browned on the second side and the fish is cooked through, about 3 minutes.

4. Serve immediately or place on a platter, cover loosely with foil, and keep warm in a 200-degree oven for up to 30 minutes.

5. Reheat the sauce gently and serve the cakes with the sauce spooned over.

Note

The easiest way to chop the peas is to pulse them in the food processor. If using frozen peas, partially thaw them before chopping.

SIMPLE GRILLED SWORDFISH WITH LEMON-CAPER BUTTER

TO ME, THE SECRET TO GRILLING SWORDFISH is a super-hot grill. There's nothing less appetizing than milky white fish, so I want to see dark-colored grill marks. I want the outside seared and the middle hot and moist. On the island, a trip to the store for exotic ingredients isn't always possible, nor is it always successful; but since I usually have a jar of capers, a stick of butter, and a lemon on hand, I make this recipe often. It's quick, simple, and delicious. *lg*

INGREDIENTS

4 TABLESPOONS (1/2 STICK) UNSALTED BUTTER

ZEST AND JUICE OF 1 LEMON

4 TABLESPOONS UNDRAINED CAPERS

4 SWORDFISH STEAKS, ABOUT 1 1/2 INCHES THICK

1 TABLESPOON OLIVE OIL

SALT AND FRESHLY GROUND BLACK PEPPER

SERVES 4

1. In a small saucepan, melt the butter over medium heat. Add the lemon zest and juice and the capers.

2. Build a hot charcoal fire or preheat a gas grill. Brush the steaks with oil and season with salt and pepper. Cook the fish, turning once, until nice dark brown grill marks appear, 4 to 5 minutes per side. The fish should no longer be translucent in the center but still moist and juicy.

3. Reheat the butter if necessary, pour over the fish, and serve.

SPICY SWORDFISH STEAKS WITH COOL CUCUMBER-CUMIN CONCOCTION

HERE'S ANOTHER GREAT RECIPE for swordfish—this one with a neat spiced cucumber topping.

Swordfish happens to be my personal all-time favorite seafood, but then I have been spoiled by years of thick swordfish steaks cut seconds after the fish have landed on deck. In general, the quality of fish to the consumer has improved drastically in the past twenty years. Commercial boats are often equipped with saltwater ice-making capability and much fish is sold at auction where the middleman sees, smells, and feels the product. Also, there is a great incentive to deliver pristine fish, because the best-quality fish commands the highest price. *lg*

INGREDIENTS

4 SWORDFISH STEAKS, ABOUT 1 1/2 INCHES THICK	1 GARLIC CLOVE, CRUSHED IN A PRESS OR MINCED
1/2 CUP PREPARED SEAFOOD SPICE RUB	1 TEASPOON GROUND CUMIN
1/2 CUP SOUR CREAM	1 TABLESPOON CHOPPED PARSLEY
1/2 CUP PLAIN FAT-FREE YOGURT	2 CUPS THINLY SLICED CUCUMBERS
1/2 CUP OLIVE OIL	SALT AND FRESHLY GROUND BLACK PEPPER
ZEST AND JUICE OF 1 LIME	1 TABLESPOON OLIVE OIL

SERVES 4

1. Rub the swordfish steaks with the spice mixture and refrigerate until ready to cook.

2. In a bowl, whisk together the sour cream, yogurt, oil, lime zest and juice, garlic, cumin, and parsley. Stir in the cucumbers and season lightly with salt and pepper. Refrigerate until ready to serve.

3. Build a hot charcoal fire or preheat a gas grill. Drizzle the fish with oil and cook, turning once, until it is no longer translucent in the center, 4 to 5 minutes per side.

4. Serve hot off the grill, topped with good dollops of the cool concoction.

Notes

There are lots of seafood spice mixtures in the spice section of the supermarket. For this dish I like one with quite a large cayenne pepper component. If the one you buy isn't spicy, add chili powder or cayenne to kick it up.

Cucumbers that are small in diameter work best here because they have fewer seeds.

STUFFED FILLET OF SOLE

I LOVE TO MAKE THIS for dinner parties, and have served it to our gourmet group several times. It's so elegant, and everyone really appreciates the effort that goes into it. By now, some of us have been in the gourmet group for almost forty years, so I hope they won't say I've overdone this one! *mg*

INGREDIENTS

8 TABLESPOONS (1 STICK) UNSALTED BUTTER

1/4 CUP CHOPPED SCALLIONS

2 GARLIC CLOVES, FINELY CHOPPED

1/4 POUND SHELLED AND DEVEINED MAINE SHRIMP, CHOPPED

1 1/2 CUPS FRESH BREAD CRUMBS

2 TEASPOONS CHOPPED FRESH DILL, PLUS SPRIGS FOR GARNISH

1 TEASPOON DRIED OREGANO

1/2 TEASPOON DRIED THYME

1/2 TEASPOON SALT

1/2 TEASPOON FRESHLY GROUND BLACK PEPPER

3 TABLESPOONS PLUS 1/2 CUP DRY WHITE WINE

SIX 6-OUNCE SOLE FILLETS

LEMON WEDGES, FOR GARNISH

SERVES 6

1. In a large skillet, heat 2 tablespoons of the butter. Add the scallions and garlic and cook over medium heat, stirring, for 2 minutes. If the shrimp are raw, add them to the skillet now and cook, stirring, until they turn pink. (If they are already cooked, just add and heat through.) Transfer to a bowl and combine with the bread crumbs, chopped dill, oregano, thyme, salt, and pepper. Moisten with the 3 tablespoons of wine, or enough to make the stuffing bind together.

2. Butter a large glass baking dish.

3. Place about 2 tablespoons of stuffing on the end of each sole fillet and roll up. Fasten with toothpicks and arrange in the baking dish, seam sides down. (The fish can be prepared up to 8 hours ahead to this point and refrigerated.)

4. Preheat the oven to 350 degrees.

5. In a small saucepan, melt the remaining 6 tablespoons of butter and add the remaining 1/2 cup wine. Pour this mixture over the fish and sprinkle with salt and pepper. Bake, uncovered, until the fish tests done and the stuffing is heated through, 15 to 20 minutes. Garnish with dill sprigs and lemon wedges and serve.

CHAPTER 4
THE BEAN POT AND COVERED DISHES

MAMA'S MAPLE-FLAVORED BAKED PEA BEANS

MY MOTHER BAKED BEANS every Saturday night, and she usually made coleslaw and hot biscuits to go with them. There were six of us children in the family and Mama let us take turns choosing which kinds of beans we'd have, which meant that I had to wait six weeks for my favorite. I liked these "little beans" or pea beans, flavored with Maine maple syrup and molasses. *mg*

INGREDIENTS

1 POUND DRIED PEA OR NAVY BEANS

1/2 CUP PURE MAPLE SYRUP

1/4 CUP PACKED LIGHT BROWN SUGAR

2 TABLESPOONS MOLASSES

1 TEASPOON DRY MUSTARD

1 1/2 TEASPOONS SALT

1/4 TEASPOON FRESHLY GROUND BLACK PEPPER

1 SMALL ONION, PEELED

ONE 1/4-POUND CHUNK SALT PORK

SERVES 10

1. Soak the beans in cold water to cover overnight.

2. Preheat the oven to 300 degrees.

3. Drain the beans and combine in a 2 1/2-quart bean pot or covered casserole with the maple syrup, brown sugar, molasses, mustard, salt, and pepper. Add the onion and salt pork. Pour enough boiling water over the beans to cover them by 1/2 inch.

4. Bake, covered, for 6 hours, or until the beans are almost tender. Check every hour or so and if the sauce is below the level of the beans, add more boiling water to cover the beans. Uncover and finish cooking for an additional 45 to 60 minutes, until the beans are tender and a rich brown and the sauce is lightly thickened.

Note

You can also make this recipe with other dried beans such as Great Northern, yellow-eyes, or Jacob's cattle.

PARMESAN RICE FOR EIGHT

THIS RICE DISH is easy to put together, and it bakes unattended in the oven, leaving you time to prepare the rest of the meal. It goes well with most anything, but I particularly like it with fish, such as Stuffed Fillet of Sole (page 95) or simple Grilled Swordfish with Lemon-Caper Butter (page 93). *mg*

INGREDIENTS

6 TABLESPOONS (3/4 STICK) UNSALTED BUTTER

3/4 CUP CHOPPED ONION

1 1/2 CUPS LONG-GRAIN WHITE RICE

3 1/2 CUPS CHICKEN STOCK

1/2 CUP FRESHLY GRATED PARMESAN CHEESE

1/2 TEASPOON SALT, OR TO TASTE

1/2 TEASPOON FRESHLY GROUND BLACK PEPPER

4 TABLESPOONS MINCED PARSLEY

SERVES 8

1. Preheat the oven to 350 degrees.

2. In a large skillet, heat the butter. Add the onion and cook over medium heat until softened, about 5 minutes. Add the rice and cook, stirring, until the rice is opaque and tinged with gold, about 3 minutes. Scrape into a 2-quart casserole dish and add the stock, cheese, salt, and pepper. Stir to combine and cover with foil.

3. Bake for 30 minutes. Add the parsley, stir again so that the rice cooks evenly, re-cover, and bake for about 30 minutes longer, or until the rice is tender. Fluff the rice, taste for seasoning, and serve.

EASY AND DELICIOUS BLACK BEAN SOUP

ALTHOUGH I LOVE ALL the old-fashioned New England dishes, sometimes I get a craving for those spicy Tex-Mex flavors. That's when I make this amazingly easy black bean soup for a quick lunch or supper. *mg*

INGREDIENTS

TWO 16-OUNCE CANS BLACK BEANS, UNDRAINED

ONE 14 1/2-OUNCE CAN CHICKEN STOCK

1/2 CUP SALSA

1 TABLESPOON CHILI POWDER

SQUEEZE OF FRESH LIME JUICE

1/2 CUP SOUR CREAM

1/2 CUP CHOPPED YELLOW ONION

1/2 CUP SHREDDED CHEDDAR CHEESE

1/4 CUP CHOPPED CILANTRO

SMALL LIME WEDGES

SERVES 4

1. Place the beans with their liquid in a large saucepan. Using a potato masher or a large fork, partially mash the beans. Whisk in the stock, salsa, and chili powder. Bring to a boil, reduce the heat to low, and simmer for about 15 minutes. Add the lime juice.

2. Serve the sour cream, chopped onion, cheese, cilantro, and lime wedges in small bowls for garnishing the soup.

Menu Selection

I KNEW FROM WATCHING TELEVISION THAT normal American families were eating spaghetti every Wednesday night. I can still hear Anthony's mother calling him home for dinner and see him running through the alleyways, dashing across streets, bolting up stairs, and plunking himself down behind an enormous mound of steaming Prince Spaghetti. He looked so happy.

Meals in the Greenlaw household were a production, too. Dinners were family time. The television and stereo were shut off and conversation was expected. My mother was quite strict about dinner etiquette and took her role as director/producer seriously. We questioned nothing and made no demands. We had absolutely no input as to the menu, not even on our birthdays. Asking my mother to prepare something for a bake sale or some school party was an insult as far as she was concerned. We knew to get a brownie mix and bake it ourselves, or buy a bag of Oreos. I can't even imagine what my mother's reaction might have been to our pouting like the little brat on TV and demanding, "I want my Maypo!" But it wouldn't have been pretty.

Blessed with a mother who thumbed her nose at culinary convention, I spent my entire childhood unaware of what day of the week it was. We aren't Catholic, so I didn't have fish to inform me of the end of the school week. I wonder how many Saturday mornings I waited at the bus stop. Why, the only semblance of a calendar I had was school lunches. The hot lunch program printed its schedule in the newspaper. It was set in stone. If I was eating a pastrami sandwich, it was Thursday.

My family went months on end never eating the same thing twice for the evening meal. (Except when Mom took Asian cooking lessons and we ate Chinese food for three months.) I suppose we must have had spaghetti once, but I'll bet it wasn't on a Wednesday. At some point

in junior high, I invited a classmate to have dinner with my family and she had the gall to ask me what my mother was serving. "I don't know and don't ask her. It'll piss her off," was my friendly warning. The classmate remembered that she needed to study for a test and begged off, which was a relief as I recalled the last time I had invited company for dinner. This friend made the mistake of inquiring, "Mrs. Greenlaw, what will we have?" before agreeing to join us. I have never forgotten Mom's response.

"You'll find out when you are asked to sit down, and I guarantee it will be better than anything that's ever been served at your house." Because I was embarrassed by my mother's remark, I didn't often invite friends for dinner. Because I knew her remark was accurate, I didn't often accept invitations to dine elsewhere.

Due to overcrowding in the elementary school in Topsham, Maine, the fourth graders were bussed to The Pejepscot School, an ancient three-room schoolhouse on the outskirts of town with dirt floors in the basement where the restrooms were. The classrooms were so cold, we girls were allowed to put our leotarded legs through the sleeves of our winter coats while sitting at our desks—and there was no hot lunch program. It was a sad and confusing year for me. I didn't have peas with mandarin oranges or fried bologna cup to mark the passage of time. My personal chef wasn't thrilled about packing lunch for me every day either, and usually sent me off with leftovers from the night before. Do you have any idea how embarrassing it is to be eating gourmet while everyone else has a soggy, cold sandwich that has been sitting in a brown bag for a minimum of six hours? The point of total humiliation came when the teacher began including my lunch in our daily show-and-tell.

As difficult as it was to confront my mother, I informed her that I would take responsibility for my own lunches for the remainder of the school year, which was several months as I recall. Much to my relief, she was delighted. I should have read the twinkle in her eye as "You'll be sorry." The lunch making became quite a challenge, as I was certain that Mom stopped buying luncheon meats, canned tuna, peanut butter, or anything else that normal kids would eat just to spite me. I assure you that I do not exaggerate when I tell you that I ate hot dog sandwiches with mustard on Wonder Bread every single noontime until that last glorious day of my fourth-grade year. I never once complained—I like hot dog sandwiches. But listening to my mother sing the jingle from the Oscar Mayer commercial every morning nearly cracked me. I almost gave in, and dreamed of the days of those little Tupperware containers filled with Chicken Marbella, Marsala, Piccata. . . . Fifth grade was a great year. Every Friday afternoon, I cut the school lunch menu for the following week out of the newspaper and taped it to the refrigerator. My world was back in order. *lg*

GINNY BREHMER'S SWEET POTATO CASSEROLE

JIM AND I LIVED IN PENNSYLVANIA for a few years and it didn't take me long to make friends with Ginny Brehmer, a fellow Mainer. Ginny was from Machias—a true Down Easter—and was a fabulous cook. She shared this delicious sweet potato casserole with me and I have made it every Thanksgiving since. *mg*

POTATOES

2 1/2 POUNDS SWEET POTATOES

4 TABLESPOONS (1/2 STICK) UNSALTED BUTTER, MELTED IF POTATOES ARE NOT HOT

1/2 CUP GRANULATED SUGAR

1/2 CUP MILK

2 LARGE EGGS

1/2 TEASPOON SALT

1/2 TEASPOON PURE VANILLA EXTRACT

PECAN TOPPING

3/4 CUP PECANS

1/2 CUP PACKED LIGHT BROWN SUGAR

3 TABLESPOONS ALL-PURPOSE FLOUR

4 TABLESPOONS (1/2 STICK) COLD UNSALTED BUTTER

SERVES 8 TO 10

1. Butter a 9 by 13-inch baking dish or other similar shallow baking dish.

2. Scrub the potatoes, cut in 2- to 3-inch chunks, and boil in salted water until tender, about 20 minutes. Drain and when cool enough to handle, peel. Mash with a potato masher (you should have about 4 cups) and beat in the butter, sugar, milk, eggs, salt, and vanilla. Spread into the prepared dish.

3. In a food processor, pulse the pecans until chopped medium fine; remove. Add the brown sugar and flour to the workbowl and process to remove large lumps. Cut the butter into chunks, add to the workbowl, and pulse until the mixture resembles coarse meal. Add the pecans and pulse once or twice just to combine. (Or you can make this topping by hand.) Sprinkle over the sweet potatoes. (The casserole can be made several hours ahead and refrigerated. Return to room temperature before baking.)

4. Preheat the oven to 350 degrees. Bake the casserole until heated through and the topping is golden, 30 to 45 minutes.

SAUSAGE AND SPINACH LASAGNA

ONE TIME, IN THE VERY DISTANT PAST, my mother had a weak moment and kindly and thoughtfully prepared and froze a huge pan of lasagna for me to take on a fishing trip. The lasagna was a great success with the crew, and although we thanked Mom profusely and plied her with fresh swordfish steaks upon our return to port, she was never inclined to repeat the gesture. I was forced to learn how to make lasagna myself, but it's never ever as good as what Mom makes. *lg*

ZIPPY TOMATO SAUCE

3 TABLESPOONS OLIVE OIL

1 YELLOW ONION, CHOPPED

6 GARLIC CLOVES, MINCED

1 TEASPOON DRIED OREGANO

1 TEASPOON DRIED BASIL

1 TEASPOON DRIED MARJORAM

3/4 TEASPOON DRIED RED PEPPER FLAKES

TWO 28-OUNCE CANS ITALIAN-STYLE TOMATOES

ONE 14-OUNCE CAN CRUSHED TOMATOES IN PURÉE

1/2 CUP DRY RED WINE

SALT AND FRESHLY GROUND BLACK PEPPER

LASAGNA

1 TABLESPOON OLIVE OIL

1 1/4 POUNDS HOT ITALIAN SAUSAGES, CASINGS REMOVED

6 1/2 CUPS ZIPPY TOMATO SAUCE

ONE 15-OUNCE CONTAINER RICOTTA CHEESE

ONE 10-OUNCE PACKAGE FROZEN CHOPPED SPINACH, THAWED AND SQUEEZED DRY

1 3/4 CUPS GRATED PARMESAN CHEESE

2 LARGE EGGS

1/4 CUP HEAVY OR WHIPPING CREAM OR HALF-AND-HALF

1/2 TEASPOON DRIED OREGANO

1/2 TEASPOON DRIED BASIL

1/2 TEASPOON FRESHLY GROUND BLACK PEPPER

9 UNCOOKED LASAGNA NOODLES

3 CUPS SHREDDED PROVOLONE CHEESE (ABOUT 12 OUNCES)

SERVES 8 TO 10

1. For the sauce, heat the oil in a large, heavy pot. Add the onion, garlic, oregano, basil, marjoram, and pepper flakes and cook over medium heat until the onion is softened, about 7 minutes. Add the Italian-style and crushed tomatoes and wine. Use the side of a spoon to break the tomatoes up into smaller pieces. Bring to a boil, reduce the heat to low, and cook, covered, stirring occasionally, for 1 1/4 hours. You should have about 9 cups. Thin with water if necessary and season to taste with salt and pepper. (The sauce can be prepared up to 2 days ahead. Cool, cover, and refrigerate.)

2. Preheat the oven to 375 degrees.

3. Make the lasagna. In a large skillet, heat the olive oil. Add the sausages and cook over medium heat

until browned, using the side of a spoon to break the meat up into coarse pieces, 10 to 16 minutes. Add the tomato sauce, bring to a boil, and simmer for 5 minutes.

4. In a large bowl, whisk together the ricotta, spinach, 1 cup of Parmesan cheese, the eggs, cream, oregano, basil, and pepper.

5. Spoon 1 cup of meat sauce into the bottom of a 9 by 13-inch baking dish. Place 3 noodles over the sauce in a single layer. Spread 1 cup of sauce over the noodles. Dollop 1 cup of the ricotta mixture over the sauce and sprinkle with 1/4 cup of the Parmesan and 1 cup of the provolone. Repeat, layering with 3 noodles, 1 cup of sauce, 1 cup ricotta mixture, 1/4 cup Parmesan, and 1 cup provolone. Arrange the remaining 3 noodles over the cheese and spoon 1 cup of sauce over. Sprinkle with the remaining 1/4 cup Parmesan and 1 cup provolone. Dollop any remaining ricotta mixture atop the lasagna and spoon the remaining sauce around the ricotta. Tightly cover the baking dish with foil.

6. Bake for 50 minutes. Uncover and continue baking until the noodles are tender and the sausage is hot and bubbly, about 25 minutes longer. Let stand for about 15 minutes before serving. (The lasagna can be made a day ahead and refrigerated. Reheat, covered with foil, in a 350-degree oven for about 40 minutes.)

7. Reheat any remaining Zippy Tomato Sauce and pass at the table if desired.

— *Note* —

You don't need to precook the noodles. I've always found that to be the most tedious part of making lasagna, so I was delighted to find out you don't necessarily need to. This recipe calls for more tomato sauce than some, which provides the extra liquid needed to soften the noodles.

CHAPTER 5
BLUEBERRIES AND CRANBERRIES

WILD BLUEBERRY PANCAKES

LET'S FACE IT: Blueberry pancakes are usually the result of a very poor blueberry-picking
expedition. I would imagine that my mother was bored to tears every time

I left the house with a bucket, promising enough berries for several pies
and returning with what made a couple of skimpy pancakes. She often
tried to pass the meager harvest off as a topping for cereal or ice cream,
but I usually insisted on pancakes. These are exceptionally light, due to the
beaten egg whites. *lg*

INGREDIENTS

4 LARGE EGGS

2 CUPS MILK

4 TABLESPOONS (1/2 STICK) UNSALTED BUTTER, MELTED

1 1/4 CUPS UNBLEACHED ALL-PURPOSE FLOUR

1 TABLESPOON SUGAR

1 TABLESPOON BAKING POWDER

1/2 TEASPOON SALT

1 CUP WILD MAINE BLUEBERRIES, RINSED

UNSALTED BUTTER

MAPLE SYRUP, PREFERABLY FROM MAINE OR VERMONT, SLIGHTLY WARMED

SERVES 6 (MAKES ABOUT 40 PANCAKES)

1. Separate the eggs, placing the yolks in one medium bowl and the whites in another bowl.
   Whisk the egg yolks with the milk and melted butter. Using an electric mixer, beat the egg
   whites to soft peaks.

2. In a large bowl, whisk together the flour, sugar, baking powder, and salt. Make a well in the center of
   the dry ingredients and add the egg/milk mixture. Whisk together gently just until blended. Don't
   worry if a few lumps remain; they will work themselves out. Fold in the egg whites and gently stir
   in the blueberries.

3. Preheat a lightly greased griddle or heavy skillet over medium heat. Ladle out the batter to form
   3-inch pancakes. Cook until bubbles appear on the top, 1 to 2 minutes, then flip and cook until
   golden brown on the bottom, about 1 minute.

4. Serve with butter and warm maple syrup.

Note

The unbleached flour in this recipe adds a slightly toasty, rich flavor. Since unbleached flour usually absorbs more liquid,
if you make these with bleached flour, add about a tablespoon more flour to the recipe.

FOGGY MORNING BLUEBERRY MUFFINS

BEAUTIFUL SUMMER MORNINGS on the island should not be spent in the kitchen, but when the cove is socked in with fog there's nothing nicer than baking up a batch of blueberry muffins and enjoying them over a leisurely breakfast at the kitchen table, watching and waiting for the fog to lift. *mg*

INGREDIENTS

1/2 CUP (1 STICK) UNSALTED BUTTER, SOFTENED

1 1/4 CUPS SUGAR

3 LARGE EGGS

1/2 CUP HALF-AND-HALF OR WHOLE MILK

3/4 TEASPOON PURE VANILLA EXTRACT

2 1/2 CUPS ALL-PURPOSE FLOUR

2 TEASPOONS BAKING POWDER

1/2 TEASPOON SALT

1 1/2 CUPS BLUEBERRIES

MAKES 18 MUFFINS

1. Preheat the oven to 425 degrees. Grease muffin tins or fit with paper liners.

2. In a large bowl, cream together the butter and sugar with an electric mixer. Beat in the eggs, half-and-half, and vanilla until the batter is smooth.

3. In a medium bowl, whisk together the flour, baking powder, and salt. Add to the egg mixture, whisking until fairly smooth. (The batter will be stiff.) Fold in the blueberries.

4. Divide among the muffin cups, filling about three-quarters full.

5. Bake for 20 to 25 minutes, until the muffins are golden brown and a skewer inserted in the center comes out clean. Cool in the tins for 5 minutes and then unmold onto a rack.

— *Note* —

Creaming the butter and sugar together creates a muffin with a very tender crumb and good keeping qualities.

MAINE BLUEBERRY PIE

DELICIOUS SMALL BLUEBERRIES GROW WILD in patches on the island. However, as Linda has

acknowledged, it's a challenge to pick enough for a pie because the deer and the birds like them, too, and often get there first and eat their fill, leaving me—if I'm lucky—only enough for muffins or pancakes. If my grandsons Aubrey and Addie are coming to visit, I make it a point to go off island and buy a couple of quarts of local native blueberries. Aubrey loves my blueberry pie, so I always make him one! *mg*

INGREDIENTS

5 CUPS BLUEBERRIES, PREFERABLY MAINE WILD
BLUEBERRIES, RINSED AND PICKED OVER

3/4 CUP SUGAR

1/4 CUP ALL-PURPOSE FLOUR

1/2 TEASPOON GROUND CINNAMON

1/2 TEASPOON GRATED LEMON ZEST

2 TABLESPOONS FRESH LEMON JUICE

1/8 TEASPOON SALT

2 TABLESPOONS (1/4 STICK) UNSALTED BUTTER, CUT IN
SMALL CHUNKS

FLAKY PIE CRUST (PAGE 226) FOR A DOUBLE-CRUST PIE,
OR PURCHASED PIE CRUSTS

MAKES ONE 9-INCH PIE

1. In a large bowl, toss the blueberries with the sugar, flour, cinnamon, lemon zest, lemon juice, and salt. Set aside while preparing the pastry.

2. Preheat the oven to 400 degrees.

3. Fit a 12-inch round of pastry dough into a 9-inch pie plate. Spoon the blueberry filling into the shell and dot with butter. Cover with the top crust and trim the overhanging dough 3/4 inch all around. Turn the edges under and crimp or flute to seal. Use a sharp knife to cut steam vents.

4. Bake until the crust is golden brown and the filling is bubbly, about 40 minutes.

LEMON-GLAZED BLUEBERRY CUPCAKES

OH, HOW I DEARLY love to make these cupcakes! The glaze that gets poured over the cakes as they finish baking becomes a deliciously sticky, slightly crunchy topping. They make a good midafternoon snack, or a great dessert after a lobster roll lunch. *mg*

BATTER

1/2 CUP (1 STICK) UNSALTED BUTTER, SOFTENED

1 1/2 CUPS GRANULATED SUGAR

2 LARGE EGGS

1/2 TEASPOON PURE VANILLA EXTRACT

2 1/4 CUPS ALL-PURPOSE FLOUR

4 TEASPOONS BAKING POWDER

1/2 TEASPOON SALT

1 CUP BLUEBERRIES (SEE NOTE)

1 CUP MILK

GLAZE

1 CUP CONFECTIONERS' SUGAR

2 TEASPOONS LEMON JUICE

1/2 TEASPOON GRATED LEMON ZEST

MAKES 2 DOZEN CUPCAKES

1. Preheat the oven to 375 degrees. Butter 24 muffin cups or fit tins with paper liners.

2. In a large bowl, beat the butter and sugar until granular with an electric mixer. Add the eggs and vanilla and beat until smooth.

3. In a medium bowl, sift or whisk together 2 cups of the flour with the baking powder and salt. Toss the blueberries with the remaining 1/4 cup of flour. On medium speed, add the flour mixture to the egg/sugar mixture, alternating with the milk. Fold in the blueberries. Spoon the batter into the muffin cups.

4. Bake for 15 minutes.

5. Meanwhile, make the glaze. In a medium bowl, whisk the sugar, lemon juice, and lemon zest with 3 tablespoons water until smooth. The glaze should be thick but spoonable.

6. After the cupcakes have baked for 15 minutes, spoon about a tablespoon of glaze over each one. Return to the oven and bake until golden brown on top and a skewer inserted in the center comes out clean, 8 to 10 minutes. Immediately run a small knife around each cupcake to loosen any sticky glaze and unmold onto a wire rack.

— *Note* —

I always use our small native "low bush" Maine blueberries, but all these recipes will also work with larger "high bush" blueberries, too.

MATTIE'S STEAMED BLUEBERRY PUDDING

WHEN OUR KIDS WERE YOUNG and we came to the island, we were all absolutely starving by the time the mail boat docked. Luckily, it was usually just in time for dinner. We walked the couple of miles from the Town Landing to the old homestead in Robinson Cove, dragging our bags filled with clothes, books, and toys. The family car was nothing if not temperamental, so we never counted on getting a ride. By this time of day, Mattie and Lil, Jim's mother and grandmother, could be found in the big kitchen, boiling lobsters and steaming our favorite blueberry pudding. The aroma of fresh biscuits wafted from the oven as we walked through the kitchen door, and we were greeted by the sight of a glass bowl on the counter filled with homemade coleslaw. Soon we were seated around the table, satisfying our hunger and happily listening to Grandpa Aub catch us up on the latest island news. *mg*

PUDDING

1 CUP GRANULATED SUGAR

4 TABLESPOONS (1/2 STICK) UNSALTED BUTTER

1/2 CUP MILK

1 LARGE EGG

1 CUP ALL-PURPOSE FLOUR

1 TABLESPOON BAKING POWDER

1/2 TEASPOON GROUND CINNAMON

1/2 TEASPOON SALT

1 TEASPOON PURE VANILLA EXTRACT

1 GENEROUS CUP MAINE BLUEBERRIES

HARD SAUCE

1/2 CUP (1 STICK) UNSALTED BUTTER, SOFTENED

2 CUPS CONFECTIONERS' SUGAR

1 TEASPOON PURE VANILLA EXTRACT

JUICE OF 1/2 LEMON

SERVES 6 TO 8

MAKES ABOUT 1 1/2 CUPS HARD SAUCE

1. For the pudding, generously butter a deep 1-quart ceramic or metal bowl.
2. In a medium bowl, beat together the sugar, butter, milk, and egg with an electric mixer until light and frothy.
3. Using a rubber spatula or whisk, blend in the flour, baking powder, cinnamon, and salt. Stir in the vanilla.
4. Spread half of the blueberries in the bottom of a heatproof 2-pint bowl. Pour the batter over the berries and spread the remaining blueberries over the top.

5. Place a folded kitchen towel or a rack in the bottom of a large saucepan. Place the bowl in the pot and add boiling water to come halfway up the sides of the bowl. Cover the pot and steam the pudding for about 1 hour, or until the pudding is firm to the touch and a skewer inserted in the center comes out clean. Cool in the covered kettle for 15 minutes and then unmold onto a platter or plate.

6. Make the hard sauce. Using an electric mixer, beat the butter and sugar together in a medium bowl until smooth. Stir in the vanilla and lemon juice. Set aside at room temperature until ready to serve on the warm pudding.

7. When ready to serve, reheat the pudding in the steamer or in a microwave. Cut into wedges and serve with hard sauce on the side.

CRANBERRY, ORANGE, AND CANDIED GINGER RELISH

CAN YOU TELL WE'RE A FAMILY THAT loves ginger in many forms? In this easy and delicious raw cranberry relish, the candied (or crystallized) ginger adds just the right sweet-hot touch. It's always on our Thanksgiving table. *mg*

INGREDIENTS

ONE 12-OUNCE BAG CRANBERRIES

1 ORANGE, UNPEELED, SEEDED, CUT INTO 1-INCH CHUNKS

3/4 CUP SUGAR

1/2 CUP (ABOUT 2 1/2 OUNCES) CHOPPED CRYSTALLIZED GINGER

1/4 CUP ORANGE MARMALADE

MAKES ABOUT 3 CUPS

1. In a food processor, coarsely chop the cranberries using on/off turns. Scrape into a bowl.

2. Coarsely chop the orange in the processor, using on/off turns, and transfer to the bowl with the cranberries. Add the sugar, ginger, and marmalade, stirring well to combine. Cover and refrigerate for at least 12 hours or up to a week. Serve cool or at room temperature.

MAMA'S BLUEBERRY BUCKLE

MAMA MADE MANY WONDERFUL old-fashioned desserts, but if I got to choose the dessert for dinner on a particular night I often requested blueberry buckle. Not only does it taste really good, but I guess I also liked the sound of its quaint, old-time name, which some say comes from the fact that the topping tends to buckle as it bakes. Mama always used Crisco, but these days I make this buckle with butter. *mg*

BATTER

1/4 CUP (1/2 STICK) UNSALTED BUTTER OR VEGETABLE SHORTENING, SUCH AS CRISCO

1/2 CUP SUGAR

1 LARGE EGG

3/4 CUP ALL-PURPOSE FLOUR

1 1/2 TEASPOONS BAKING POWDER

1/2 TEASPOON SALT

1/3 CUP MILK

2 CUPS MAINE BLUEBERRIES

TOPPING

1/2 CUP SUGAR

1/3 CUP ALL-PURPOSE FLOUR

1 TEASPOON GROUND CINNAMON

6 TABLESPOONS (3/4 STICK) UNSALTED COLD BUTTER

WHIPPED CREAM OR YOUR FAVORITE WHIPPED TOPPING

SERVES 6 TO 8

1. Preheat the oven to 350 degrees. Butter an 8-inch square baking dish.

2. In the bowl of an electric mixer, cream the butter and sugar until light and fluffy. Add the egg and mix until combined.

3. In a small bowl, sift or whisk together the flour, baking powder, and salt. Add the dry ingredients to the batter, alternating with the milk, mixing until smooth and blended.

4. Scrape the batter into the prepared pan and spread with a rubber spatula so that it evenly covers the pan. Sprinkle the berries over the batter.

5. To make the topping, whisk together the sugar, flour, and cinnamon in a small bowl. Add the butter and work with a fork or your fingers until the mixture is crumbly. (You can also do this in a food processor.) Sprinkle the crumb topping over the blueberries. Bake for about 40 minutes, or until the berries are bubbling and the topping is golden brown.

6. Serve warm, with whipped cream or your favorite whipped topping.

CRANBERRY-PEAR CRISP WITH ALMOND TOPPING

IF YOU'VE NEVER THOUGHT OF putting cranberries and pears in the same dish, you'll be especially pleased with this dessert. This crisp is particularly good served for dessert following an autumn dinner such as the Pork Tenderloin Medallions with Caramelized Apples (page 143) or the Braised Chicken with Garlic and Fennel (page 153). *mg*

INGREDIENTS

5 CUPS PEELED AND SLICED FIRM PEARS, SUCH AS BOSC OR BARTLETT (ABOUT 2 POUNDS)

2 1/2 CUPS (8 OUNCES) WHOLE CRANBERRIES

1 1/2 CUPS GRANULATED SUGAR

1/2 CUP PACKED LIGHT BROWN SUGAR

1/2 CUP ALL-PURPOSE FLOUR

1/2 CUP (1 STICK) COLD UNSALTED BUTTER, CUT IN SEVERAL CHUNKS

1 CUP OLD-FASHIONED OR QUICK-COOKING ROLLED OATS (NOT INSTANT OATMEAL)

1/2 CUP SLICED ALMONDS

VANILLA ICE CREAM

SERVES 8 TO 10

1. Butter a shallow 2 1/2- to 3-quart baking dish. Preheat the oven to 350 degrees.

2. In a large bowl, toss the pears with the cranberries and granulated sugar. Spread in the bottom of the prepared dish.

3. In a food processor, process the brown sugar and flour to remove any lumps in the sugar. Add the butter and pulse until the mixture resembles coarse meal. Add the oats and almonds and pulse once or twice just to combine. (You can also mix the topping by hand.) Sprinkle over the fruit, spreading to make an even layer.

4. Bake, uncovered, in the preheated oven until the pears and cranberries are tender and the topping is browned, 50 minutes to 1 hour.

5. Serve hot or warm with scoops of ice cream.

Note

The crisp can be reheated in a 400-degree oven for about 10 minutes.

CAPE COD CRANBERRY-NUT BREAD

OF COURSE CAPE COD IS WELL KNOWN for its cultivated cranberries, but they are native to Maine, too. In the fall, when we're walking in the fields, we often come across secret small boggy patches where the wild cranberries live. The plants grow low to the ground, and the beautiful smallish berries hide under their russet-colored leaves. It's fun to gather a few handfuls—sometimes just about enough to make a loaf of this cranberry-nut bread. *mg*

INGREDIENTS

2 1/2 CUPS ALL-PURPOSE FLOUR

1 1/4 CUPS SUGAR

2 TEASPOONS BAKING POWDER

1/2 TEASPOON BAKING SODA

1/2 TEASPOON SALT

1 LARGE EGG

1/2 CUP ORANGE JUICE

1/4 CUP LEMON JUICE

2 TABLESPOONS VEGETABLE SHORTENING OR UNSALTED BUTTER, MELTED

1 1/2 CUPS COARSELY CHOPPED CRANBERRIES

1/2 CUP CHOPPED WALNUTS OR PECANS

MAKES 1 LOAF

1. Butter a medium-sized loaf pan. Preheat the oven to 350 degrees.

2. In a large bowl, sift or whisk together the flour, sugar, baking powder, baking soda, and salt. In another bowl, whisk the egg with the orange juice, lemon juice, and melted shortening.

3. Pour the liquid ingredients into the dry ingredients and stir gently but thoroughly to blend. Fold in the cranberries and nuts. Scrape into the prepared pan and bake for about 1 1/4 hours, or until a skewer inserted in the center comes out clean. Cool in the pan on a rack for 15 minutes; unmold onto a rack and cool completely before slicing. (This bread is even better when wrapped and refrigerated for a day before slicing. It also freezes well.)

Note

You can chop cranberries by hand, using a large knife, or by pulsing in a food processor. Do not overprocess—you want some chunks, not a purée.

Thanksgiving

MY FOURTH-GRADE TEACHER, Mrs. Bran, was compelled to dampen our spirits on my favorite holiday by spending the week leading up to it lecturing and testing us on the cold, hard facts of the history of Thanksgiving. While kindergarten through third-grade teachers spent the third week in November making gumdrop turkeys and construction paper pilgrim hats, Mrs. Bran's no-nonsense lessons overshadowed any of the fun previously associated with the holiday. The years may have eliminated a few of the details and perhaps distorted the accuracy, but here's what I remember:

In the year 1620, 104 pilgrims landed at Plymouth Rock after a harrowing sixty-six-day crossing of the North Atlantic Ocean. The first few months in the New World saw the pilgrims dwindle to a sparse fifty in count as sickness, disease, and starvation killed men, women, and children. The brave and noble leader of the Wampanoags, Squanto, befriended the pilgrims' Captain Miles Standish and literally saved what was left of the newcomers by teaching them to hunt, fish, and plant corn. Healthy pilgrims began to thrive and invited Squanto and his family to a celebratory feast—the very first Thanksgiving. When Squanto arrived with ninety of his closest relatives, it was clear that the pilgrims were overwhelmed and undersupplied, so the Native Americans went back to their wigwams to get food to contribute to the pilgrims' meager stores for the planned three-day feast. They soon returned with a herd of deer, a flock of turkeys, fish, corn, beans, squash, and berries. It was quite a party. But, alas, the peace and friendship deteriorated. The next generation of pilgrims, hosting the hostile gene, was intolerant of the Indian ways and customs and began killing the peace-loving natives in some number while engaging in King Phillip's War. Bows and arrows were no match for rifles. In time, the white men managed to usurp most of the land and kill all of the buffalo, leaving the Native Americans in a state of despair and hopelessness.

A normally happy-go-lucky and well-adjusted fourth grader, I was deeply affected by these facts, and the only way I had to overcome the guilt and cope with history was to embrace and embellish the rumor of a hint of Indian blood in the Greenlaw line. I clearly recall lying to everyone about my heritage. Fortunately, my coloring allowed for at least my school chums to believe that my great-grandmother was a "full-blooded Abenaki." I fabricated so many details that I began to believe the story myself. Previously a huge fan of Daniel Boone, my new hero was Mingo. When some math whiz pointed out that my percentage of Abenaki blood was well beneath 25, I owned up to another 25 percent of Penobscot blood that was not usually discussed because of some scandal of which details were sketchy.

Today, the Greenlaws celebrate Thanksgiving in the tradition shared by most New Englanders. It's a gathering of friends and family all of whom contribute something to the feast centered around the biggest turkey available. We begin planning the holiday just after the Fourth of July fireworks—it's far bigger than Christmas. The usual thirty or so folks who celebrate Thanksgiving in my family's home are thankful for good health, abundant food, family, and friends. We do a lot of toasting. But in the back of my mind, the "truth" lingers. To take this to its logical conclusion: Only I know that we have overcome tremendous odds and survived certain doom. We are a proud people. Thanksgiving is my favorite holiday, and I have Mrs. Bran to thank for that. *lg*

SIMON'S FAVORITE NEW ENGLAND SALAD WITH BERRIES AND GOAT CHEESE

WE EAT A LOT OF SALADS—mostly because we enjoy them, but also for health reasons. This one is a particular favorite and we like the fact that it's made with some of the best local New England ingredients, including the maple syrup, cranberries, and goat cheese. It makes a great first course or is substantial enough to be a light meal by itself. You can vary the amounts of ingredients to suit your taste. *lg*

MUSTARD-MAPLE VINAIGRETTE

3 TABLESPOONS BALSAMIC VINEGAR

1 TABLESPOON REAL MAPLE SYRUP

1 TEASPOON DIJON MUSTARD

1/2 CUP OLIVE OIL

SALT AND FRESHLY GROUND BLACK PEPPER

SALAD

4 TO 6 CUPS SEASONAL GREENS

ABOUT 20 SUGAR SNAP PEAS

2/3 CUP FRESH BLUEBERRIES

2/3 CUP DRIED CRANBERRIES

2/3 CUP TOASTED WALNUTS

2/3 CUP CRUMBLED LOCAL GOAT CHEESE

SERVES 4

1. For the dressing, whisk together the vinegar, maple syrup, and mustard in a small bowl. Whisk in the oil and season with salt and pepper to taste.

2. Spread the greens on a platter or individual plates. Top with the sugar snaps, berries, walnuts, and cheese, drizzle with the vinaigrette, and serve.

CHAPTER 6

MEAT AND POULTRY

BEEF TENDERLOIN STUFFED WITH LOBSTER

THIS IS ABSOLUTELY THE MOST DECADENT "surf and turf" you'll ever experience. My mother prepares this recipe once a year—usually for Christmas dinner—and it's a real treat. *lg*

TENDERLOIN

6 BACON SLICES

ONE 3 1/2- TO 4-POUND WHOLE BEEF TENDERLOIN, TRIMMED

MEAT FROM 2 COOKED LOBSTER TAILS, HALVED LENGTHWISE

1 1/2 TEASPOONS FRESH LEMON JUICE

1 TABLESPOON UNSALTED BUTTER, MELTED

SAUCE

1 CUP (2 STICKS) UNSALTED BUTTER

1/2 CUP SLICED SCALLIONS

2 GARLIC CLOVES, MINCED

1 CUP DRY WHITE WINE

2 TEASPOONS CHOPPED FRESH TARRAGON

SERVES 6

1. Preheat the the oven to 425 degrees.

2. In a skillet, heat the bacon over medium heat just until partially cooked. Do not let the bacon turn crisp. Remove and drain on paper towels. Reserve.

3. Cut the tenderloin lengthwise almost through so that you can butterfly it. Leave about 1/2 inch and open the tenderloin like a book. Lay the lobster meat along the split tenderloin.

4. In a small bowl, stir together the lemon juice and melted butter. Drizzle this over the lobster meat. Close the tenderloin around the lobster and tie together securely with kitchen twine at 1-inch intervals.

5. Put the tenderloin on a rack in a roasting pan and roast for about 30 minutes. Check the internal temperature with an instant-read thermometer. About 5 minutes before it's done, lay the reserved bacon slices on top. Return to the oven and continue roasting just until the bacon crisps and the meat is done. When the tenderloin reaches 125 to 130 degrees and you want it medium-rare, remove it from the oven. Let the tenderloin rest for about 15 minutes, during which time its temperature will rise to about 140 degrees, or medium-rare. Remove the bacon and slice the meat for serving.

6. Meanwhile, in a saucepan, melt 2 tablepoons of butter over medium heat. Reduce the heat to low and sauté the scallions and garlic for 3 to 4 minutes, or until softened but not colored. Add the remaining butter and the wine, raise the heat to medium, and cook until the butter melts and the sauce is hot. Stir in the tarragon and cook for 2 to 3 minutes for the flavor to develop.

7. Arrange the slices of tenderloin on a warm platter and spoon the butter sauce over it.

BEEF WITH GUINNESS

I CONFESS TO BEING a little apprehensive the first time I made this stew because I wasn't sure about the prunes and almonds. As it turned out, I loved it and my husband Jim raved about it. He attributed the good flavor to the Guinness. You can decide for yourself! *mg*

INGREDIENTS

2 TABLESPOONS VEGETABLE OIL

2 BAY LEAVES

2 POUNDS BEEF CHUCK, CUT INTO 1-INCH CUBES AND PATTED DRY

1 LARGE ONION, SLICED

2 TABLESPOONS ALL-PURPOSE FLOUR

1/2 CUP STOUT, PREFERABLY GUINNESS

8 OUNCES CARROTS, SLICED

1/2 CUP MINCED PARSLEY

SALT AND FRESHLY GROUND BLACK PEPPER

4 OUNCES PITTED PRUNES

4 TO 5 OUNCES ALMONDS, TOASTED

SERVES 6 TO 8

1. Preheat the oven to 300 degrees.

2. Heat the oil and bay leaves in a Dutch oven over medium heat. When hot, start browning the meat in 2 or 3 batches, taking care not to crowd the pan. As each batch of meat browns, remove the pieces with tongs and set aside on a plate. They should be lightly colored on all sides. Add the onion to the pan and cook for 4 to 5 minutes, or until lightly browned and softened.

3. Return the meat to the pan, reduce the heat to low, and sprinkle the flour over it. Cook, stirring, for about 3 minutes, or until the flour is absorbed. Mix in the stout and 1/2 cup water, bring to a simmer over medium heat, and add the carrots and parsley. Season to taste with salt and pepper, cover, and transfer to the oven. Bake for 1 1/2 hours. Stir the stew several times during baking.

4. Add the prunes and almonds and cook for about 30 minutes longer, or until the meat is tender and cooked through. Remove the bay leaves before serving.

MARTHA'S BEEF STIFADO

I USE A SLOW COOKER (or Crock-Pot) to make this stifado, which is a traditional Greek stew usually made with beef and whatever else the cook deems tasty (or has nearby). I usually make braises such as this in the oven or on top of the stove, but this one is a winner in the slow cooker—and so easy when you need to save time by assembling the stew and then letting it cook all day long. *mg*

INGREDIENTS

3 TABLESPOONS UNSALTED BUTTER OR OLIVE OIL

2 1/2 POUNDS STEWING BEEF, SUCH AS CHUCK OR ROUND, CUT INTO 1-INCH CUBES AND PATTED DRY

16 OUNCES FROZEN OR JARRED PEARL ONIONS, DRAINED IF JARRED

1 TABLESPOON LIGHT BROWN SUGAR

1/2 CUP DRY RED WINE

3 TABLESPOONS TOMATO PASTE

1/4 CUP RED WINE VINEGAR

1 TEASPOON PICKLING SPICE

4 WHOLE CLOVES

3 GARLIC CLOVES, MINCED

1 TEASPOON SALT

ONE 10-OUNCE PACKAGE FROZEN PEAS, THAWED

SERVES 8

1. Heat the butter or oil in a large, deep skillet over medium heat. When hot, start browning the meat in 2 or 3 batches, taking care not to crowd the pan. As each batch of meat browns, remove the pieces with tongs and transfer to a slow cooker. They should be lightly colored on all sides.

2. Put the onions in the skillet and sprinkle with brown sugar. Cook over medium heat for 10 to 12 minutes, or until the onions are lightly glazed. Transfer to the slow cooker.

3. Add the wine, 1/2 cup water, the tomato paste, and vinegar to the skillet, raise the heat to medium-high, and cook, stirring with a wooden spoon to scrape all the brown bits into the sauce. Pour over the meat and onions.

4. Lay a piece of cheesecloth on the countertop and put the pickling spice and cloves in the center. Gather the sides together and tie with kitchen twine. Put the bouquet garni in the slow cooker. Add the garlic and salt and secure the lid on the slow cooker.

5. Cook on low, 200 degrees, for 8 hours.

6. Thirty minutes before the stew is done, add the peas to the pot and continue cooking.

Note

You can follow this recipe using a Dutch oven on top of the stove. Once the stew ingredients are in the pot (through step 4), transfer the covered Dutch oven to a 300-degree oven and cook for about 2 1/2 hours. Add the peas and cook for 20 to 30 minutes longer.

THREE-ALARM MAINE CHILI

WHEN WE WANT SOMETHING to warm us up on chilly, foggy days, I make this long-cooking chili

and keep it hot on the back of the stove. It has a kick to it, but you could adjust the heat by only using one or two cherry peppers. Serve this with the Red Pepper and Cheddar Cornbread (page 195). *mg*

INGREDIENTS

1 POUND STATE OF MAINE KIDNEY BEANS OR ANY DRY RED KIDNEY BEANS

2 POUNDS GROUND BEEF CHUCK

1 MEDIUM ONION, CHOPPED

1 LARGE GARLIC CLOVE, MINCED

ONE 28-OUNCE CAN CHOPPED OR DICED TOMATOES, WITH THEIR JUICE, OR 4 LARGE FRESH TOMATOES, CORED AND CHOPPED

ONE 8-OUNCE CAN TOMATO SAUCE

4 MEDIUM-HOT CHERRY PEPPERS, CHOPPED (SEEDS AND ALL)

2 TABLESPOONS CHILI POWDER

SALT AND FRESHLY GROUND BLACK PEPPER

SERVES 8

1. In a large bowl, soak the kidney beans in enough cold water to cover for 4 to 6 hours. Drain and replace the water once or twice during soaking.

2. Drain the beans and transfer to a large pot. Add enough cold water to cover and bring to a boil over high heat. Reduce the heat to medium-high and simmer rapidly for about 45 minutes, or until the beans are tender. Drain off most of the liquid and set the beans aside.

3. In a large Dutch oven or similar pot, brown the beef over medium-high heat, stirring until it loses its pinkness. Lift from the pot with a slotted spoon and set aside. Drain off all but about 2 tablespoons of fat.

4. Add the onion and garlic to the pot and cook for 6 to 8 minutes, or until the onion is translucent and soft. Return the beef to the pot and add the tomatoes, tomato sauce, cherry peppers, and chili powder. Stir well and season to taste with salt and pepper. Add the beans and stir well to mix.

5. Cover and simmer over medium heat for 2 1/2 to 3 hours, or until the chili is rich and full flavored. Adjust the seasonings and serve hot. The chili won't be harmed by longer cooking or by being kept hot over low heat for several hours.

CHICKEN PASTIES

THIS IS ONE OF MY FAVORITE WAYS to use up leftover chicken. It's very rich but tastes just delicious on cool days and is a good alternative to chicken sandwiches for lunch or to any casual meal. Because I use store-bought crescent dinner rolls, it couldn't be easier! *mg*

PASTIES

TWO 3-OUNCE PACKAGES CREAM CHEESE, SOFTENED

2 TABLESPOONS (1/4 STICK) UNSALTED BUTTER, SOFTENED

2 CUPS DICED COOKED CHICKEN

2 TABLESPOONS MILK

1 TABLESPOON CHOPPED ONION

1 TABLESPOON CHOPPED PIMIENTO

1/2 TEASPOON SALT

1/8 TEASPOON BLACK PEPPER

TWO 8-OUNCE CANS REFRIGERATED CRESCENT DINNER ROLLS

MELTED UNSALTED BUTTER

1 TABLESPOON FRESH OR DRIED BREAD CRUMBS

SAUCE

ONE 10 3/4-OUNCE CAN CREAM OF MUSHROOM SOUP

1 CUP SOUR CREAM

1/4 CUP MILK OR CHICKEN STOCK

1/4 CUP CHOPPED PIMIENTOS

SERVES 4

1. Preheat the oven to 350 degrees.
2. To make the pasties, blend the cream cheese with the butter in a mixing bowl, mashing it with a fork until smooth. Add the chicken, milk, onion, pimiento, salt, and pepper and mix well.
3. Separate the dough into eight rectangles and divide the chicken mixture equally in the center of each rectangle. Gather the four corners of each rectangle up and over the center of the filling and pinch the dough together to seal into a bundle. Arrange on two ungreased baking sheets.
4. Brush each pasty with melted butter and sprinkle with the bread crumbs.
5. Bake for 20 to 25 minutes, or until the pasties are lightly browned and the filling is hot.
6. To make the sauce, combine the soup, sour cream, milk or stock, and pimientos in a large saucepan. Heat over medium heat until hot.
7. Serve the pasties with the mushroom sauce spooned over them.

CURRIED SHEPHERD'S PIE

WHEN I AM IN THE MOOD for something warming on a cold winter night—like tonight, when snow  is in the forecast—I love to make this curried shepherd's pie. Depending on who is having dinner with us (and what I have in the freezer), I use lean ground beef or ground lamb. It is delicious and satisfying with either, and can be made a few hours ahead of time and put in the oven when you're ready. *mg*

INGREDIENTS

6 RUSSET (BAKING) POTATOES, ABOUT 2 POUNDS, PEELED AND CUT INTO CHUNKS

SALT

1 TABLESPOON VEGETABLE OIL

3/4 CUP FINELY CHOPPED ONIONS

1 TABLESPOON FINELY MINCED GARLIC

1 OR 2 TABLESPOONS CURRY POWDER

1 TEASPOON GROUND CUMIN

1 TEASPOON GROUND CORIANDER

2 POUNDS LEAN GROUND BEEF

1 CUP CRUSHED CANNED IMPORTED TOMATOES

1/2 CUP HOMEMADE OR CANNED CHICKEN OR BEEF STOCK

1 TEASPOON SUGAR

FRESHLY GROUND BLACK PEPPER

1/2 CUP MILK, WARMED UNTIL HOT

3 TABLESPOONS UNSALTED BUTTER

2 CUPS COOKED FRESH OR FROZEN PEAS

SERVES 6

1. Preheat the oven to 375 degrees.

2. Put the potatoes into a large saucepan, add enough cold water to cover, sprinkle generously with salt, and bring to a boil over high heat. Reduce the heat and cook for 25 to 30 minutes, or until the potatoes are tender to the core when pierced with a fork.

3. Meanwhile, in a large, deep skillet, heat the oil over medium-low heat. Add the onions and garlic and cook, stirring occasionally, for about 5 minutes, or until they are soft. Take care the garlic does not burn. Stir in the curry powder, cumin, and coriander and cook briefly just until fragrant.

4. Add the meat and cook, stirring with a wooden spoon to break it up, until it loses most of its pink color. Add the tomatoes, stock, and sugar and season to taste with salt and pepper. Cook, stirring occasionally, for 20 to 30 minutes, or until cooked through and the flavors blend.

5. Drain the potatoes. Put them through a food mill or potato ricer or mash them with a potato masher or fork. Return them to the same pan, which should still be a little hot. Add the hot milk, 2 tablespoons of the butter, and season to taste with pepper. Beat with a wooden spoon until well mixed.

6. Stir the peas into the beef mixture and heat briefly. Transfer the beef to a 2-quart baking dish or casserole. Top with the mashed potatoes and smooth them over the beef. At this point, the casserole can be refrigerated until you are ready for the final cooking.

7. Dot with the remaining tablespoon of butter and bake for about 30 minutes (or longer if the casserole has been refrigerated), or until the potatoes are golden brown and the filling is bubbling hot.

GRILLED PORK TENDERLOIN WITH ROASTED RED PEPPERS

THIS RECIPE IS FUN because it is one that Mom and I do together, usually for a crowd. Mom does all of the prep work while I am responsible only for grilling the pork. If my mother does not enjoy the idea of an activity, she simply refuses to learn how to do it (pumping gas is one example). Mom is convinced that she would not enjoy standing outside, swatting mosquitoes, inhaling smoke, and staring at the grill, so grilling has become my part, making this the perfect recipe for a joint to-do. The juicy slices of tenderloin surrounded by the red pepper are a very festive and delicious centerpiece for a party meal. *lg*

INGREDIENTS

TWO 12-OUNCE JARS LARGE ROASTED RED PEPPERS OR
6 LARGE RED PEPPERS, ROASTED (SEE NOTE)

1 1/4 CUPS OLIVE OIL

1/2 CUP GOLDEN RAISINS

3 TABLESPOONS BALSAMIC VINEGAR

2 LARGE GARLIC CLOVES, MINCED

SALT AND FRESHLY GROUND BLACK PEPPER

1 1/2 CUPS CHOPPED SCALLIONS (5 OR 6 SCALLIONS)

1/2 CUP BOTTLED BARBECUE SAUCE (YOUR FAVORITE)

1/3 CUP WHITE WINE VINEGAR

3 TABLESPOONS LIGHT SOY SAUCE

2 TABLESPOONS PACKED LIGHT BROWN SUGAR

1 TABLESPOON JALAPEÑO SAUCE

1 TABLESPOON HONEY

2 TEASPOONS WORCESTERSHIRE SAUCE

4 POUNDS PORK TENDERLOIN, TRIMMED OF EXCESS FAT

SERVES 8

1. Drain the peppers and rinse under cool running water. Drain well, then slice the peppers into thin strips. Transfer to a mixing bowl and add 1/4 cup of olive oil, the raisins, balsamic vinegar, and garlic. Season to taste with salt and pepper. This may be prepared ahead of time and refrigerated for up to 24 hours. Let the peppers stand at room temperature for 2 hours before using.

2. In another mixing bowl, combine the remaining 1 cup of olive oil with the scallions, barbecue sauce, vinegar, soy sauce, brown sugar, jalapeño sauce, honey, and Worcestershire sauce. Mix well.

3. Put the pork in a glass or ceramic baking dish and pour the marinade over. Refrigerate for at least 2 hours and up to 12 hours.

4. Prepare a charcoal or gas grill until the coals or heating elements are medium hot.

5. Lift the pork tenderloins from the marinade and let the marinade drip back into the dish. Lay the tenderloins on the grill and cook for about 20 minutes, turning often with tongs, until cooked through and an instant-read thermometer inserted in the thickest part registers 150 degrees.

6. Transfer the pork to a cutting board and let it rest for about 5 minutes, during which time the internal temperature will rise to 155 degrees.

7. Slice the pork and arrange it on a serving platter. Spoon the pepper sauce around it and serve.

Note

To roast whole peppers on the grill, put them over the hot coals or heat source and cook until the skin begins to turn black and char. Turn with tongs and grill until charred all over. You can accomplish the same thing under a broiler or over an open flame. When charred, transfer the peppers to a paper bag or bowl, cover, and let them cool until you can rub off the blackened skin without burning your fingers. Cut them open and scrape out the seeds. Proceed with the recipe.

GRILLED BUTTERFLIED LEG OF LAMB

MY SON CHUCK is a wonderful cook and a true master of the grill. He and my son-in-law Ben are better

at it than any two people I know and it's always fun to watch the "grill boys" in action. It's not unusual for them to have two or three grills going at once.

At my request Chuck will go to Pat's Meat Market in Portland, Maine, and pick up a boneless leg of lamb when he's coming to visit us on the island. The next day, he lets the lamb marinate so that by evening it's ready to grill. I guess I don't have to tell you it's the best lamb I have ever had.

You can't adopt my son, but you are welcome to his recipe! *mg*

INGREDIENTS

1/2 CUP DRY SHERRY

1/2 CUP BRANDY

2 MEDIUM ONIONS, ROUGHLY CHOPPED

10 LARGE GARLIC CLOVES, PEELED

1 TEASPOON SALT

1/2 TEASPOON FRESHLY GROUND BLACK PEPPER

1 TEASPOON GROUND CUMIN

1 TEASPOON DRIED ROSEMARY OR TWO 3-INCH SPRIGS, LEAVES REMOVED

ONE 5- TO 6-POUND BUTTERFLIED LEG OF LAMB

SERVES 6 TO 8

1. In a small saucepan, combine the sherry and brandy and heat over medium heat until hot. Very carefully—and standing back from the stove—ignite the alcohol with a match. Let it burn until it extinguishes itself. If you don't do this, the alcohol will flare on the grill. Let the sherry and brandy cool to room temperature.

2. In a blender, purée the onions, garlic, salt, pepper, cumin, and rosemary. Add the cooled alcohol.

3. Put the lamb in a nonreactive roasting pan or glass dish large enough to hold it and pour the marinade over it. Turn the lamb several times to coat evenly with the marinade. Cover and refrigerate for at least 8 hours and up to 24 hours.

4. Prepare a charcoal or gas grill until the coals or heating elements are medium hot or preheat the broiler.

5. Meanwhile, lift the lamb from the marinade. Pat dry with paper towels and set it aside for about 15 minutes to come to cool room temperature. Discard the marinade unless you want to use it as a sauce.

6. Lay the leg of lamb on the grill and cook for 25 to 30 minutes, turning two or three times, until evenly browned and cooked through. An instant-read thermometer inserted in the thickest part of the meat will register 135 degrees for medium-rare lamb. The time will depend on the heat of the grill and the thickness of the meat. Transfer the lamb to a cutting board and let it rest for about 5 minutes before slicing.

7. If you want to use the marinade as a sauce, boil it for at least 5 minutes over high heat and serve warm. Pass the sauce on the side with the sliced lamb.

PORK TENDERLOIN MEDALLIONS WITH CARAMELIZED APPLES

PORK AND APPLES JUST GO TOGETHER and when fall arrives on the island, I braise tenderloins with some good apples. I like Granny Smiths, but you could use any firm, crisp apples. Those from a local orchard will taste best, and of course all through New England we have wonderful orchards where you can pick your own or buy them from the side of the road. *mg*

INGREDIENTS

2 PORK TENDERLOINS, EACH ABOUT 1 POUND, TRIMMED OF EXCESS FAT AND SLICED INTO 3/4-INCH-THICK MEDALLIONS (ROUNDS)

SALT AND FRESHLY GROUND BLACK PEPPER

2 TABLESPOONS (1/4 STICK) UNSALTED BUTTER

3 TABLESPOONS OLIVE OIL

2 MEDIUM-SIZED FIRM, TART APPLES, SUCH AS GRANNY SMITHS, PEELED, CORED, AND SLICED INTO ROUNDS OR WEDGES ABOUT 1/2 INCH THICK

2 LARGE GARLIC CLOVES, FINELY MINCED

1 CUP DRY VERMOUTH

1/4 CUP DIJON MUSTARD

2 TABLESPOONS SOY SAUCE

1 TABLESPOON GRATED LEMON ZEST

SERVES 4 TO 6

1. Preheat the oven to 325 degrees. Butter a baking dish large enough to hold the medallions in a single layer and set aside.

2. Season the medallions on both sides with salt and pepper.

3. In a large, heavy skillet, melt the butter, add the olive oil, and heat over medium-high heat until very hot. Sear the medallions, a few at a time, until browned on both sides. As each one is browned, transfer to the baking dish in a single snug layer.

4. In the same skillet, sauté the apple slices for about 5 minutes over medium heat, turning once or twice. Add more butter if necessary. Using tongs or a spatula, transfer the apples to the baking dish and layer them over the pork.

5. Add the garlic to the pan and cook for about 1 minute over medium heat. Add the vermouth, mustard, soy sauce, and zest, bring to a simmer, and simmer for about 5 minutes, scraping the bottom of the pan with a wooden spoon to remove the browned bits. Pour over the pork and apples.

6. Cover the baking dish tightly with aluminum foil and braise for 25 to 30 minutes on the center rack of the oven, or until the pork is cooked through.

CROWN ROAST OF PORK WITH CRANBERRIES

A CROWN ROAST OF PORK is made from two center racks of ribs connected and formed into a circle. You may be more familiar with a crown roast of lamb, but one made from pork racks is equally succulent and impressive—and less costly. Call well ahead and ask the butcher to form the crown for you. The crown roast with the cranberry stuffing is festive, making it a good choice for the holidays. *mg*

INGREDIENTS

1 CUP (2 STICKS) UNSALTED BUTTER	1/2 CUP SUGAR
8 CUPS 1/4-INCH BREAD CUBES (ABOUT 12 SLICES)	1 TEASPOON DRIED MARJORAM
4 TABLESPOONS GRATED ONION	1 TEASPOON DRIED THYME
2 GARLIC CLOVES, MINCED	2 TEASPOONS SALT
3 CUPS CHOPPED RAW CRANBERRIES (ONE 12-OUNCE BAG)	FRESHLY GROUND BLACK PEPPER
1 CUP DRY WHITE WINE	ONE 13- TO 14-POUND CROWN ROAST OF PORK (ABOUT 18 RIB CHOPS)

SERVES 6

1. Preheat the oven to 325 degrees.

2. In a large skillet, melt the butter over medium heat. Add the bread cubes, onion, and garlic and sauté for about 10 minutes, or until the bread is lightly browned and the butter is absorbed.

3. Add the cranberries, wine, sugar, marjoram, thyme, and salt. Season to taste with pepper; I usually give it about 10 turns of the mill. Spoon the stuffing into the center of the roast.

4. Cover the tips of the roast with aluminum foil to prevent burning and roast for 1 3/4 to 2 hours, or until an instant-read thermometer inserted in the meatiest part of a chop registers 150 to 155 degrees. Begin checking the temperature at 1 hour and 40 minutes; you don't want to overcook the meat. The stuffing should register about 160 degrees. Remove the aluminum foil about 15 minutes before the roast is done. Let the roast rest for at least 20 minutes, tented with foil to keep it warm. If the stuffing needs further cooking, remove it from the roast during resting and return to the oven until it's hot in the center. Spoon it back into the roast for serving.

5. Serve by slicing between the ribs. Serve each rib chop with a spoonful of stuffing or remove the stuffing and pass it on the side.

LAMB SHISH KEBABS

DURING THE EARLY YEARS OF OUR MARRIAGE, Jim and I and our two older daughters, Rhonda and Linda, lived in Waterville, Maine. We had Armenian neighbors with two little boys who played with the girls. Linny, being a tomboy, was always ready for a game of Daniel Boone and more times than not was Daniel Boone himself—she had the raccoonskin hat to prove it! Gimella, the boys' mother, was a first-rate cook and it was from her that I learned to make lamb shish kebab, our family favorite. *mg*

INGREDIENTS

5 TABLESPOONS OLIVE OIL

4 TABLESPOONS LEMON JUICE

2 TABLESPOONS CHOPPED ONION

2 TEASPOONS CURRY POWDER

1 1/2 TEASPOONS SALT

1 TEASPOON CORIANDER SEEDS

1 TEASPOON GROUND GINGER

1 GARLIC CLOVE, CHOPPED

3 POUNDS LEAN, BONELESS LAMB, FROM THE SHOULDER, LEG, OR SIRLOIN, CUT INTO 1 1/2-INCH CUBES

12 FRESH PEELED, FROZEN, OR JARRED PEARL ONIONS (SEE NOTE)

18 LARGE CHERRY TOMATOES

18 LARGE WHITE MUSHROOMS, STEMS REMOVED

EIGHTEEN 1-INCH-THICK ZUCCHINI SLICES

SERVES 6

1. In a shallow glass, ceramic, or other nonreactive dish, combine the olive oil, lemon juice, onion, curry powder, salt, coriander seeds, ginger, and garlic. Add the lamb, toss to coat, and cover. Alternatively, mix the marinade in a sturdy plastic bag, add the cubes, seal, and gently turn the bag to coat the meat. Refrigerate for at least 4 hours and up to 8 hours, stirring or turning occasionally.

2. Prepare a charcoal or gas grill until the coals or heating elements are medium hot or preheat the broiler.

3. Lift the lamb from the marinade and let any excess marinade drip back into the dish. Thread the lamb onto 6 metal skewers, alternating with the onions, cherry tomatoes, mushrooms, and zucchini.

4. Lay the skewers on the grill or under the broiler about 4 inches from the heat. Cook for 3 to 4 minutes on each side for medium-rare meat or longer for more well-done meat and until the vegetables soften. Move the skewers to cooler or hotter parts of the grill during cooking to avoid burning. Baste once with the marinade in the first minutes of grilling or broiling.

5. Serve immediately, a skewer per serving.

--- *Note* ---

If you use fresh onions, peel and then parboil them for 3 or 4 minutes just until they begin to turn tender. Drain and cool.

BRAISED LAMB SHANK WITH DRIED APRICOTS

JUST READING THE INGREDIENTS in this makes me want to get into the kitchen and start cooking. Everything I like is in this dish. During its two hours in the oven, my house fills with marvelous aromas. Serve mashed potatoes with it to soak up every bit of the juice. *mg*

INGREDIENTS

3 TABLESPOONS CUMIN SEEDS

3 TABLESPOONS CORIANDER SEEDS

FOUR 12- TO 14-OUNCE LAMB SHANKS, TRIMMED OF EXCESS FAT

SALT AND FRESHLY GROUND BLACK PEPPER

1/4 CUP OLIVE OIL

2 CARROTS, CHOPPED

2 CELERY RIBS, CHOPPED

1 LARGE YELLOW ONION, GRATED

ONE 1-INCH FRESH GINGER KNOB, PEELED AND FINELY CHOPPED

LARGE PINCH OF SAFFRON

1 CUP WHITE WINE

1 CUP WHOLE DRIED APRICOTS (ABOUT 6 OUNCES)

1 1/2 TEASPOONS GROUND CLOVES

1 TEASPOON GROUND GINGER

2 BAY LEAVES

1 CINNAMON STICK

4 CUPS HOMEMADE OR CANNED CHICKEN STOCK

1/2 CUP SESAME SEEDS

1/4 CUP CHOPPED DRIED APRICOTS (ABOUT 1 1/2 OUNCES)

1 TABLESPOON UNSALTED BUTTER

SERVES 4 TO 6

1. Preheat the oven to 350 degrees.

2. In a small skillet, toast the cumin seeds over medium heat for about 1 minute, or until fragrant and lightly browned. Stir a few times during toasting. Transfer to a spice grinder or mortar and add the coriander seeds. Grind or crush with a pestle. Set aside.

3. Season the lamb shanks with salt and pepper.

4. In a large roasting pan, heat the oil over medium-high heat and brown the lamb shanks for 10 to 15 minutes, or until lightly browned on all sides. Set the shanks aside.

5. Pour off all but about 1 tablespoon of the fat and add the carrots and celery to the pan. Cook over medium heat for 4 to 5 minutes, or until the vegetables begin to soften. Add the onion, fresh ginger, and saffron, and cook for about 5 minutes, or until the onion is translucent. Add the wine, whole apricots, cloves, ground ginger, bay leaves, cinnamon stick, and reserved cumin and coriander. Cook for about 5 minutes, stirring until fragrant.

6. Return the shanks to the pan and add the stock. Cover and roast for about 3 hours, or until the meat is tender and falling off the bone. Remove the lamb and keep it warm, covered with foil.

7. Skim the fat from the pan drippings and then strain the liquid into a saucepan. Discard the solids. Reduce the braising liquid by simmering it gently over medium heat for 10 to 20 minutes, or until it reaches a saucy consistency. The time will vary depending on the pan and the intensity of the heat. Add the sesame seeds and chopped apricots and then swirl in the butter. Adjust the seasonings with salt and pepper.

8. Pull the meat off the shank bones and arrange on a platter. You may leave it on the bone, but it's easier to serve off the bone. Ladle the sauce over the lamb shanks.

CHICKEN PIE WITH HERB BISCUITS

MY FRIEND NANCY SUMMERS on Isle au Haut. During the past twenty years, she and her husband Bill have "camped" in the park (about half of the island is part of Acadia National Park), rented most of the available houses, and finally were able to buy some land, a coup that is almost unheard of on the island. We happily watched them build their beautiful home, met their entire families on both sides, and by now count them among our closest friends. When Nancy gave me this recipe for chicken potpie and told me it was one her mother used to make, I was delighted. It's delicious and I know you will like it, too. *mg*

FILLING

8 BONELESS, SKINLESS CHICKEN BREAST HALVES

1 1/2 CUPS LIGHT CREAM

3 CARROTS, PEELED AND DICED

2 ZUCCHINI, DICED BUT NOT PEELED

1 TABLESPOON UNSALTED BUTTER

1/2 YELLOW ONION, DICED

2 TABLESPOONS MINCED GARLIC

6 TABLESPOONS ALL-PURPOSE FLOUR

2 1/2 CUPS HOMEMADE OR CANNED CHICKEN STOCK

1/2 CUP COGNAC OR WHITE WINE

1 CUP FROZEN PEAS

3 TEASPOONS DRIED TARRAGON

1 TEASPOON SALT

FRESHLY GROUND BLACK PEPPER

BISCUITS

2 CUPS ALL-PURPOSE FLOUR

1 TABLESPOON BAKING POWDER

1 TABLESPOON SUGAR

3/4 TEASPOON SALT

1/2 CUP (1 STICK) COLD UNSALTED BUTTER, DICED

3/4 CUP HALF-AND-HALF

1 TEASPOON DRIED TARRAGON

1 TEASPOON DRIED DILL

2 TABLESPOONS (1/4 STICK) UNSALTED BUTTER, MELTED

SERVES 8 TO 10

1. Preheat the oven to 350 degrees.

2. Make the filling. In a baking dish large enough to hold the chicken breast halves in a slightly overlapping layer, arrange the chicken breasts and then pour the cream over them. Bake for 20 to 25 minutes, or until the chicken is just cooked through. Do not turn off the oven.

3. Remove the chicken from the dish. Reserve the cream and pan juices. When the chicken is cool enough to handle, cut it into bite-sized pieces and set aside.

4. In a large saucepan of boiling water, blanch the carrots over medium-high heat for 3 minutes. Add the zucchini and cook for 3 minutes longer. Drain the vegetables and set aside.

5. In a large frying pan, melt the butter over low heat and gently sauté the onion for 3 to 4 minutes. Add the garlic and cook about 2 minutes longer. Add the flour, stirring constantly, and cook for about 5 minutes until lightly browned and the flour loses its floury taste. Slowly add the stock, stirring constantly.

6. Stir in the Cognac and the reserved cream and pan juices and continue to cook over low heat for 6 to 7 minutes, or until heated through and the flavors blend.

7. Remove the pan from the heat and stir in the peas, reserved carrots and zucchini, chicken, and tarragon. Season with the salt and pepper to taste. Transfer to a baking dish large enough to hold the mixture easily and bake for 15 to 20 minutes, or until the vegetables are fork-tender.

8. Meanwhile, make the biscuits. In a mixing bowl, whisk together the flour, baking powder, sugar, and salt. Add the cold, diced butter and using your fingers, a pastry blender, or a fork, work the butter into the dry ingredients until the pieces of butter are the size of small peas.

9. Add the half-and-half, tarragon, and dill and stir just until mixed.

10. Turn the dough out onto a lightly floured surface and knead four or five times until the dough holds together. Roll or pat the dough into a circle about 1/4 inch thick. Using an upturned glass or a biscuit cutter, cut out circles about 2 1/2 inches in diameter.

11. When the chicken mixture has cooked for 15 or 20 minutes, remove the dish from the oven and lay the biscuits over the filling so that the circles overlap just enough to cover the filling. A few gaps is fine.

12. Brush the biscuits with the melted butter and return the pan to the oven for 20 to 25 minutes, or until the biscuits are lightly browned and the filling is bubbling.

TURKEY STUFFING

USE THIS TO STUFF YOUR TURKEY OR DO AS I DO: Bake it in a casserole alongside the turkey as it roasts. *mg*

INGREDIENTS

2 TABLESPOONS VEGETABLE OIL

3 CUPS CHOPPED CELERY

2 CUPS CHOPPED ONIONS

1 POUND BULK COUNTRY SAUSAGE

2 TART APPLES, PEELED, CORED, AND CUT INTO 1/2-INCH CUBES

1 CUP HAZELNUTS, TOASTED, SKINNED, AND CHOPPED

1 CUP DRIED CHERRIES

6 CUPS STALE BREAD CUBES (ABOUT 12 BREAD SLICES)

1 TEASPOON SALT

1 TEASPOON DRIED THYME LEAVES

1 TEASPOON CRUMBLED DRIED SAGE LEAVES

FRESHLY GROUND BLACK PEPPER

1 CUP TAWNY PORT

1 CUP HOMEMADE OR CANNED CHICKEN STOCK

MAKES ABOUT 6 CUPS, ENOUGH FOR ONE 10- TO 12-POUND TURKEY

1. Preheat the oven to 325 degrees.

2. In a large skillet, heat the oil over medium heat. Add the celery and onions and sauté for about 10 minutes, or until soft. Transfer to a large bowl.

3. Add the sausage to the skillet and cook for about 10 minutes, or until lightly browned, and add to the bowl. Stir in the apples, hazelnuts, and cherries. Add the bread cubes and toss lightly. Sprinkle with the salt, thyme, sage, and pepper. Stir in the port and chicken stock.

4. Transfer the stuffing to a buttered casserole dish or put the stuffing in the turkey's cavity.

5. Bake the stuffing for 40 to 50 minutes, or until heated all the way through. Serve with the turkey.

Note

You can stuff this into the cavity of a 10- to 12-pound turkey. Make sure the center of the stuffing reaches 170 degrees. Insert an instant-read thermometer into the center of the stuffing inside the turkey to determine its temperature.

BRAISED CHICKEN WITH GARLIC AND FENNEL

THIS RECIPE IS A LITTLE MORE WORK THAN I am usually willing to put forth in the kitchen, but my mother will occasionally make this as a special request. Requests for certain dishes are something my mother has grown tolerant of only in her more mature years. A request for any particular recipe during her more feisty middle age ensured that we might never see that meal again— independence to the nth degree! This Braised Chicken with Garlic and Fennel is so good that Mom has, in her very recent past, humored her husband's and middle daughter's subtle hints and suggestions that we might find it tasty on a cold winter evening. It's great as a leftover too! This is perhaps my favorite recipe in this book. I love it! *lg*

INGREDIENTS

2 LARGE GARLIC HEADS

3 FENNEL BULBS, ABOUT 1 1/2 POUNDS TOTAL

TWO 3- TO 3 1/2-POUND CHICKENS, EACH CUT INTO 8 PIECES (WINGS RESERVED FOR ANOTHER USE), OR 12 PIECES BONE-IN CHICKEN PARTS

ALL-PURPOSE FLOUR, FOR DUSTING

SALT AND FRESHLY GROUND BLACK PEPPER

8 TABLESPOONS OLIVE OIL

3 CARROTS, PEELED AND CUT INTO 1/2-INCH-THICK SLICES

2 STRIPS ORANGE ZEST, EACH ABOUT 2 1/2 INCHES LONG AND 1/2 INCH WIDE

1 TEASPOON FENNEL SEEDS

1 POUND NEW POTATOES, EACH ABOUT 1 1/2 INCHES IN DIAMETER, SCRUBBED CLEAN, OR CUT TO SIZE IF LARGE

1/2 CUP WHITE WINE

2 CUPS HOMEMADE OR CANNED CHICKEN STOCK

SERVES 6

1. Preheat the oven to 350 degrees.

2. Remove the papery outer skin from the garlic heads and separate the cloves. Peel the cloves but leave them whole (about 20 cloves).

3. Chop enough feathery fronds from the fennel to measure 1 tablespoon and reserve for garnish. Trim the fennel stalks (fronds) flush with the bulbs and discard the stalks. Halve the bulbs and remove the cores. Cut the fennel into 1/2-inch-thick slices.

4. Skin the chicken or leave the skin on, depending on your preference. Dust the chicken lightly with flour and season lightly with salt and pepper.

5. In a large Dutch oven, heat 2 tablespoons of oil. Working in batches, brown the chicken, cooking on each side for 1 1/2 to 2 minutes, or until lightly browned. As they brown, lift the chicken parts from the pan with tongs and set aside. Add oil as needed. You will use about 6 tablespoons of oil to brown all the chicken.

6. Discard the oil. Return the pan to the heat and add the remaining 2 tablespoons of oil. Add the carrots, orange zest, fennel seeds, peeled garlic cloves, and fennel. Season to taste with salt and pepper. Cook over medium heat, stirring gently, for about 5 minutes, or until the carrots begin to soften. Add the potatoes and wine, raise the heat slightly, and cook, stirring gently and scraping up any browned bits on the bottom of the pan. Add about 2 teaspoons of salt and 1 teaspoon of pepper.

7. Add the chicken and stock, cover tightly, and bake for about 1 hour and 15 minutes, or until the chicken is cooked through and the vegetables are tender. Stir in the reserved fennel fronds and serve immediately.

MOM'S BEST CHICKEN SALAD

I SERVE MY FAMILY THIS SALAD for lunch many times during the summer. It makes enough for 12 and even so, there are usually leftovers waiting in the 'fridge for Jen, my daughter-in-law, to snack on after her daily run. *mg*

INGREDIENTS

1 QUART HOMEMADE OR CANNED CHICKEN STOCK

8 CELERY RIBS, TRIMMED

1 ONION, QUARTERED

FEW SPRIGS OF FLAT-LEAF PARSLEY

12 SKINLESS, BONELESS CHICKEN BREAST HALVES
(SEE NOTE)

1 LARGE DILL PICKLE, FINELY CHOPPED

ONE 3 1/2-OUNCE JAR CAPERS, UNDRAINED

1/2 CUP APPLE CIDER VINEGAR

1/4 CUP SAFFLOWER, CANOLA OR OTHER VEGETABLE OIL

SALT AND FRESHLY GROUND PEPPER

ABOUT 1 CUP MAYONNAISE

LETTUCE

FOR GARNISH

BLACK OLIVES

GREEN OLIVES

DEVILED EGGS OR SLICED HARD-COOKED EGGS

CHERRY TOMATOES

SERVES 12

1. In a large skillet or similar pan, bring the stock to a simmer over medium-high heat. Add 2 celery ribs, the onion, and the parsley. Add the chicken breasts and poach for about 20 minutes, or until nearly white in color and cooked through. Lift the chicken from the poaching liquid and set aside to cool. Discard the poaching liquid.

2. Chop the remaining 6 celery ribs fine.

3. When the chicken is cool enough to handle, shred it or chop it fine.

4. In a mixing bowl, mix the chicken with the chopped celery, dill pickle, and capers.

5. In a small bowl, whisk together the vinegar and oil. Season to taste with salt and pepper and pour over the chicken salad. Cover and refrigerate for at least 2 hours or overnight.

6. Drain the chicken salad of most of the liquid. Add mayonnaise to taste and serve on lettuce leaves. Garnish with olives, eggs, and cherry tomatoes.

Note

I often make this with 6 whole bone-in chicken breasts. They require about twice the amount of time to poach. Let them cool, then remove the skin and bones before proceeding with the recipe.

CITRUS-SCENTED ROAST TURKEY

THANKSGIVING IS MY FAVORITE HOLIDAY and I have fond memories of the big day on the island. When we all gathered, as we did every year, it was a sight to behold. Besides the six of us, there was Jim's sister Sally and her husband, Charlie, plus their kids, John, Tom, Suzy, Dana, and Dianne. My sister Gracie, her husband, Bud, and daughter Cindy would come and bring two widow ladies, Esther and Hazel. My sister Avis brought her son Randy. Jim's brother George came alone in those days, being the family bachelor. I think that adds up to about thirty for dinner.

We set up two tables, one large one in the kitchen for all the rowdy kids and one in the dining room for all the rowdy grown-ups. This meant double dishes of everything.

A typical menu would include large platters of Maine shrimp cocktail and Sweet and Spicy Roasted Nuts (page 34) to eat before the meal. When we sat down, we always began with a squash soup that was followed by roast turkey, Turkey Stuffing (page 151), Glazed Bittersweet Onions (page 191), Peas and Turnips with Dill Butter (page 183), Roasted Root Vegetables with Thyme and Marjoram Vinaigrette (page 170), Ginny Brehmer's Sweet Potato Casserole (page 107), Make-Ahead Party Potatoes (page 187), gravy, and a few cranberry relishes. Dessert would include Thanksgiving Pumpkin Pie with Walnut Crust (page 223), Bibo's Pumpkin Squares (page 217), Island Apple Pie (page 226), Maine Blueberry Pie (page 116), and usually a pecan pie and a chocolate cream pie.

We would have such a wonderful day that no one went home until late in the evening. By that time I had made turkey soup, so they ate again before they left. The next Thanksgiving we would do it all over again, except it would be at Sally's house. More or less the same people, and certainly the same number.

Now that I am a senior citizen my son Chuck is having the Thanksgiving dinner. He is a great cook, and it seems as though it takes no effort on his part. There will be the same number of people, just a few different faces. *mg*

INGREDIENTS

ONE 10- TO 12-POUND TURKEY, AT ROOM TEMPERATURE

SALT AND FRESHLY GROUND BLACK PEPPER

2 CELERY RIBS, CUT INTO 2-INCH LENGTHS

1 ONION, QUARTERED

1 ORANGE, QUARTERED

1 LEMON, QUARTERED

3 FLAT-LEAF PARSLEY STEMS

1 BAY LEAF

4 TABLESPOONS (1/2 STICK) UNSALTED BUTTER, AT ROOM TEMPERATURE

1 CUP HOMEMADE OR CANNED CHICKEN STOCK

SERVES 10 TO 12

1. Position a rack in the middle of the oven and preheat the oven to 425 degrees. Oil a V-shaped rack and set it in a roasting pan.

2. Remove the gizzard and heart from the turkey and discard or reserve for another use. Rinse the turkey with cold water, inside and out, and pat dry with paper towels. Season the cavity with salt and pepper. Put the celery, onion, orange, lemon, parsley stems, and bay leaf in the cavity. Rub the outside of the bird with the butter and sprinkle with salt and pepper.

3. Place on the rack in the pan, breast side down, and roast for 40 minutes, basting with the pan juices after 20 minutes. Turn the breast right side up and add the stock to the pan. Reduce the heat to 325 degrees and continue to roast for 2 1/2 to 3 1/4 hours longer, basting every 15 to 20 minutes with the pan juices, until the turkey is golden and cooked through.

4. Start testing for doneness after 2 hours; an instant-read thermometer inserted into the thickest part of the breast away from the bone should read 160 degrees. Alternatively, insert it into the thickest part of the thigh and it should read 170 degrees. The juices will run clear and the legs will feel loose when wiggled.

5. Let the turkey rest for about 30 minutes before removing the vegetables and fruit from the cavity. Carve the turkey and serve with the stuffing on page 151.

Wild Turkey

MY BEST FRIEND ALDEN WAS BETWEEN HOSPITAL STAYS during the fall of his two-year bad spell preceding surgery, pacemaker, and the total revision of the myriad of prescription medications that finally put him back on his feet. Not feeling well enough to put in full days hauling lobster traps, nor poorly enough to simply remain in bed, he decided (with some coaxing from me) to come out to the island for a short visit.

He arrived on the early boat in bright sunshine and blustery wind wielding a clam hoe over his head as the boat was made fast to the float. "Just in time to turn over the flats," Alden exclaimed, noting the level of the tide, which was indeed low. By the time he reached the top of the ramp connecting float to pier, Alden was less enthusiastic, entirely out of breath, and offered a sad apology for his health. Perhaps digging clams was too ambitious for my friend today, I realized, and I suggested a turkey hunt instead. "I'm not up to chasing a stupid bird around this damned rock," Alden spat as he climbed into my truck.

Assuring him that there would be no "chase," I pulled the 22-caliber rifle from under the seat and laid it between us as I drove slowly off the dock and headed away from the activity surrounding the daily mail run. "We may not get anything, but it's a beautiful day. We'll at least enjoy the process!" I said cheerily, hoping to arouse some interest in my friend.

"To hell with the process! Let's put some meat on the table."

We hadn't gone far, maybe less than half a mile, when I saw a small group of mature turkeys pecking at something in the grass not far off the road and conveniently on my side. I stopped the truck, rolled down the driver's side window, and took careful aim at the large tom closest to me. Just before squeezing the trigger, I heard Alden chuckle and whisper, "Heater hunting . . . I love it," referring to the style of stalking prey in which the predator never leaves the vehicle.

"BANG!" I tried to mask my surprise at my own marksmanship when the turkey dropped to its chest. Expecting the bird to skitter around like the proverbial chicken, I jacked the empty cartridge from the gun and put a new shell into the chamber ready for another shot to finish the job. The only thing that moved was Alden. He sprang from the truck, gleefully cheering, "Nice shot! Fresh turkey for dinner!" Before I could think and act responsibly by removing the fresh kill from my neighbor's front lawn, thereby escaping any eyewitness accounts of hunting out of season and without a license, Alden was standing over the bird with a knife in his pawlike hand. He gingerly nudged the turkey with the toe of his rubber boot half expecting, I could tell, the turkey to jump to its feet and do the death scramble. The turkey lay still. "Dead as a mitten! Right in the neck. What a shot!" I wished Alden would keep his voice down, and told him so, to which he replied, "Do you think anyone heard the gunshot?" He was right, I thought. I was being paranoid, but I continued to look nervously around just the same. While Alden plucked, gutted, and beheaded the turkey, I prayed no one would happen upon the scene of the crime. He was quick. The clean carcass was in the basket originally intended for clams in the back of the truck and we were nearly at my driveway when we met the only vehicle since leaving the dock. We exchanged friendly waves and I sighed an audible "Phew" as we rounded the turn toward home, believing we had narrowly escaped what could have been awkward at best.

I rinsed the turkey in my kitchen sink, and threw it first into a roasting pan, then into the oven, convincing myself that no one on the island would really miss a single turkey—even though this particular bird had been corn fed as Alden discovered during the disembowelment. As the bird cooked, Alden and I played cribbage, rehashed many old hunting and fishing adventures, and were generally pleased with our fruitful expedition that morning. Although less strenuous than digging clams, the turkey hunt resulted in the desired effect. We were actively feeding ourselves. Life had purpose. "No excuse for anyone going hungry . . ." Alden was almost smug.

We made a trip to the general store as the turkey continued to roast, buying some items to round out this early Thanksgiving meal, since I had originally planned clam chowder for the evening's menu. Potatoes, a can of cranberry sauce, and a winter squash that appeared to have resided here longer than some members of the year-round population were placed on the counter next to the cash register. I resisted the temptation to buy a mountain of unnecessary ingredients to throw off any suspicion the cashier might harbor. "Looks like someone is planning a turkey dinner," Sue MacDonald mentioned casually as she bagged the groceries. Before I could say something to the effect of "chicken," Alden replied with an affirmative—the truth, the whole truth, and nothing but the truth. He didn't miss a single detail and was delighted to refer to me as Annie Oakley. I felt my cheeks flush. In what I believed to be a ploy for a little female attention, Alden added that we couldn't dig clams due to his physical condition, to which Sue responded that digging clams was not allowed presently as the flats had been closed for red tide. Much to my relief, Sue did not bat an eye at the illegal turkey hunt, but rather stated that she would like to know if we enjoyed the bird as she intended to try one herself.

The indicator on the door of my 1926 Glenwood range had reached 300 degrees. The warmth had filled the entire kitchen, and the aroma of roasting turkey extending all the way to the front door warmed Alden and me as much as the temperature as we reentered the house with the bag of groceries. Alden stretched out on the couch and was soon snoring as I peeled, boiled, and mashed potatoes and squash. It certainly wouldn't be a fancy meal, but the basics alone were an appropriate tribute to our celebration of the right to feed oneself in the hunter-gatherer tradition. Alden and I had historically agreed on few things; the right to feed ourselves regardless of regulations and permits never stirred an argument between us. Alden was right, I mused as I set the table for two: Anyone who lives on the coast of Maine and is somewhat ambulatory should never starve. There are blueberries, mackerel, and lobster as far as the eye can see in season, and clams and mussels year-round—all to be harvested for consumption without the firing of a single shot.

Alden awoke with a stretch and a yawn and happily stated that he had enjoyed "a good kink." I decided that the turkey must be done by now and searched for oven mitts while Alden sharpened a knife for the carving. My mouth watered in anticipation as I opened the oven door.

Something didn't look quite right, but the old range didn't have a light, so I reached in and pulled the bird from the darkness and into full view. The Butterballs my mother produced always came out of the oven with their legs relaxed and politely crossed at the ankles. Not this bird. Its legs stood straight up in the air, spread-eagled, like those of a dead animal in a children's cartoon. Alden and I both began to laugh at this strange-looking bird. "It looks surprised," Alden giggled. We tried to play another game of cribbage while the bird cooled enough to carve, but I couldn't stop laughing long enough to count to thirty-one, so we gave up and decided to eat before someone dropped in and saw this ridiculous turkey.

Alden, a self-proclaimed drumstick man, helped himself to one of the legs that had been severed while I served myself a thick slice of breast meat. Alden sank his teeth into the well-browned and steaming leg with a quiet and satisfied "mmmm." He appeared to have a little trouble actually achieving a bite of meat, so he withdrew his teeth and tried again. And then again. Placing the drumstick back on his plate unscathed, Alden said, "It's tougher than a boiled owl." I didn't question the credibility of this comparison coming from a man who admits to having eaten horsemeat during the Depression and claims it "tasted just like the whinny."

One bite of white meat sent me to the sink for drinking water with one word on my mind: sawdust. Alden tried a piece of the breast and asked for some gravy or au jus, of which there was not a drop. Alden's last attempt was a wing. "Eating it *should* be the easy part," he laughed as he tossed the unharmed wing back to the platter. We ate vegetables and cranberry sauce until we were sated, but not really satisfied. The day had surely become a lesson in the importance of enjoying the process, for we had certainly not enjoyed the goal once achieved. I put the platter of turkey into the refrigerator and vowed to make soup, which was surprisingly delicious. *lg*

LINDA'S TURKEY SOUP

THE ONLY TIME I make turkey soup, other than after the event written about in "Wild Turkey" on page 158, is following Thanksgiving. I usually make so much that I eat it for a week and do not care to see it again for another year. I have substituted lentils for the rice I use here and enjoyed the variation very much. I also like to squeeze a wedge of lemon or lime into the bowl before serving if the batch happens to come out on the spicier side. *lg*

INGREDIENTS

CARCASS OF A ROASTED 10- OR 12-POUND TURKEY (OR LARGER)

HOMEMADE TURKEY OR CHICKEN STOCK OR CANNED CHICKEN STOCK (SEE NOTE)

1 1/2 POUNDS TURNIPS, PEELED AND CUT INTO 1/2 -INCH CUBES

6 MEDIUM CARROTS, PEELED AND CUT INTO 1/2 -INCH SLICES

4 LARGE CELERY RIBS, CHOPPED

2 MEDIUM ONIONS, CHOPPED

1/2 CUP WILD RICE

2 TABLESPOONS FINELY CHOPPED FRESH ROSEMARY

2 TABLESPOONS FINELY CHOPPED FRESH THYME

PINCH OF MACE

PINCH OF CUMIN

SALT AND FRESHLY GROUND BLACK PEPPER

2 CUPS SUGAR SNAP PEAS, CUT INTO BITE-SIZED PIECES

2 TO 3 CUPS COOKED AND CUBED TURKEY (SEE NOTE)

SERVES 6

1. Put the turkey carcass in a large soup pot and add enough cold water to cover. Bring to a boil over high heat and immediately reduce the heat. Cover and simmer for about 2 hours. Strain the stock and discard the bones. Return the stock to the pot.

2. Add the canned chicken stock to the pot so you have about 12 cups (3 quarts) of liquid. Add the turnips, bring to a simmer over medium heat, and cook for about 15 minutes, or until the turnips begin to soften.

3. Add the carrots, celery, onions, and rice and simmer 20 minutes longer, or until the rice is partially cooked. Stir in the rosemary, thyme, mace, and cumin. Taste and season with salt and pepper.

4. Simmer gently over medium-low heat for about 30 minutes longer, or until the vegetables are tender and the rice is cooked through.

5. Add the sugar snap peas and the cooked turkey meat about 5 minutes before serving so the peas can cook and the meat heats up. Serve hot.

Note

Making turkey soup is an inexact science. The amount of stock and the amount of turkey meat that ends up in the soup depends on the size of the turkey carcass and how much meat is left on it to cut into cubes. However, you will need at least 10 to 12 cups of liquid.

PETEY'S OVERNIGHT CHICKEN SALAD

WHEN I INVITED MY GOURMET GROUP to the island one weekend, my friend Petey brought along this salad for lunch the next day. Everyone loved the combination of chicken, sprouts, water chestnuts, and the mild curry dressing. It's best made the night before. *mg*

INGREDIENTS

6 CUPS SHREDDED ICEBERG LETTUCE

4 OUNCES BEAN SPROUTS

1 CUP SLICED WATER CHESTNUTS

1 MEDIUM CUCUMBER, PEELED AND THINLY SLICED

1/2 CUP THINLY SLICED SCALLIONS

4 CUPS SLICED COOKED CHICKEN (ABOUT 2-INCH-WIDE STRIPS), SEE NOTE

ONE 9- OR 10-OUNCE PACKAGE FROZEN SUGAR SNAP PEAS OR SNOW PEAS, THAWED AND PATTED DRY

4 CUPS MAYONNAISE

4 TEASPOONS CURRY POWDER

2 TABLESPOONS SUGAR

1 TEASPOON GROUND GINGER

SALT AND FRESHLY GROUND BLACK PEPPER

24 CHERRY TOMATOES, SLICED

1 CUP LIGHTLY SALTED PEANUTS

SERVES 10 TO 12

1. In a shallow, 4-quart rigid plastic container or similar dish, distribute the shredded lettuce in an even layer. Top with layers of bean sprouts, water chestnuts, cucumber slices, and scallions. Layer the chicken on top and then layer the snow peas on top of the chicken.

2. In a small bowl, stir together the mayonnaise, curry powder, sugar, and ginger. Season to taste with salt and pepper. Spread the dressing evenly over the snow peas and cover the dish with its lid or plastic wrap. Refrigerate for at least 2 hours until chilled and up to 24 hours.

3. Just before serving, top with the sliced tomatoes and peanuts. Scoop down into the salad for each serving.

Note

For 2 cups of sliced cooked chicken, begin with about 14 ounces of uncooked chicken. Leftover chicken is great, but I sometimes cook a couple of chicken breasts just to make this.

VENISON MINCEMEAT

DURING HUNTING SEASON in northern New England, the wonderful aroma of venison mincemeat cooking on the back of the stove emanates from kitchens up and down the coast and far into the interior.

Early in the hunting season, my mother would start begging for a neck of deer to make mincemeat, and one of my big brothers was always happy to oblige. I never knew if she was convinced that the neck had the best flavor, or if she thought she stood a better chance of getting a neck from hunters—steaks and roasts were the preferred cuts. Anyhow, as soon as she got a neck, she would go about making huge amounts of mincemeat and putting it up in pint jars. We would have delicious, warm mincemeat pies through the Thanksgiving and Christmas seasons.

Although I do not have my mother's recipe, I was so happy to receive this one from Grace Leeman of Orr's Island, Maine, a wonderful and well-known cook, and a great storyteller, too. Thank you, Grace! *mg*

INGREDIENTS

ABOUT 4 POUNDS VENISON MEAT

2 POUNDS SUET

8 POUNDS APPLES, PEELED, CORED, AND QUARTERED

2 QUARTS APPLE CIDER

1 QUART GRAPE JUICE

4 POUNDS RAISINS

3 POUNDS CURRANTS

3 POUNDS SUGAR

2 CUPS MOLASSES

1 TABLESPOON GROUND CINNAMON

1 TABLESPOON GROUND CLOVES

1 TEASPOON FRESHLY GRATED NUTMEG

1 TEASPOON SALT

1 TEASPOON PEPPER

MAKES ABOUT 4 QUARTS

1. In a very large pot, cover the venison and suet with enough water to cover by an inch or two and bring to a boil over high heat. Reduce the heat and cook until the venison is just tender when pierced with a knife. Add more water if necessary to keep the meat covered during cooking.

2. Remove the pot from the heat and let the meat and suet cool in the cooking liquid. The surface fat will harden. Scrape it off and discard.

3. Remove the meat and suet and chop both into small pieces. Transfer to a large mixing bowl.

4. Return the pot to the heat and bring the cooking liquid to a boil over high heat. Reduce the heat slightly and cook at a rapid simmer for 20 to 25 minutes, or until the liquid reduces to 1 1/2 cups. (The time will depend on the amount of water you begin with.)

5. Chop the apple quarters and add them to the chopped venison and suet.

6. Add the rest of the ingredients as well as the reduced cooking liquid. Mix well and then bring the mixture to a rapid simmer over medium-high heat. Immediately reduce the heat to low and cook gently for 2 hours, stirring often, until all the ingredients are soft and blended.

7. Let the mincemeat cool. Transfer to containers with lids and refrigerate for up to 1 week. The mincemeat freezes beautifully. Put it in quart-sized freezer containers, the perfect amount for a single pie.

GRILLED SPICED HENS

I LOVE TO GRILL THESE LITTLE HENS for a casual summer party. Everyone gets their own hen,

which is grilled so that the outside is crisp and the inside moist and sweet. How could you go wrong? If the hens you buy are on the large size, and if you have a lot of other food at the meal, you might be able to serve a few more people than six. *mg*

INGREDIENTS

6 CORNISH GAME HENS, ABOUT 1 TO 1 1/4 POUNDS EACH

2 TABLESPOONS PAPRIKA

2 TABLESPOONS CHILI POWDER

4 TEASPOONS GARLIC POWDER

1 TEASPOON CELERY SALT

1/2 TEASPOON SALT

1/2 TEASPOON DRY MUSTARD

1/2 TEASPOON CAYENNE

1/3 CUP SAFFLOWER, CANOLA, OR OTHER VEGETABLE OIL

SERVES 6

1. Halve the hens with a large, heavy knife, or have your butcher halve them for you. Rinse the halves and pat dry with paper towels.

2. In a small bowl, mix together the paprika, chili powder, garlic powder, celery salt, salt, mustard, and cayenne. Add the oil and mix well. Brush or rub the spice mixture over all the sides of the hens, working it into the meat.

3. Transfer to a dish, cover, and refrigerate for at least 1 hour or up to 6 hours. Let the hens sit at room temperature for about 15 minutes to come to room temperature before grilling.

4. Prepare a charcoal or gas grill until the coals or heating elements are medium hot.

5. Grill the hen halves, bone side up, on an uncovered grill directly over the coals for 20 minutes. Turn and grill for 10 to 20 minutes more, or until the juices run clear when pierced with a fork or small knife and an instant-read thermometer inserted in the meat near the thigh registers 170 to 175 degrees.

CHAPTER 7

FROM THE GARDEN

ROASTED ROOT VEGETABLES WITH THYME AND MARJORAM VINAIGRETTE

THIS COLORFUL VEGETABLE DISH looks great next to the turkey and cranberry sauce at Thanksgiving, but don't let that stop you from making it anytime you want roasted vegetables. And it's so easy; you can make it well ahead of time and serve it either warm or at room temperature. *mg*

INGREDIENTS

9 TABLESPOONS EXTRA-VIRGIN OLIVE OIL

2 TABLESPOONS PLUS 1 1/2 TEASPOONS CHOPPED FRESH THYME

2 TABLESPOONS PLUS 1 1/2 TEASPOONS CHOPPED FRESH MARJORAM

2 POUNDS YAMS, PEELED, HALVED LENGTHWISE, AND CUT CROSSWAYS INTO 1 1/4- TO 1 1/2-INCH PIECES

1 1/2 POUNDS CARROTS, PEELED AND CUT INTO 3/4 -INCH ROUNDS (ABOUT 4 CUPS)

1 1/2 POUNDS PARSNIPS, PEELED AND CUT INTO 3/4 -INCH-THICK ROUNDS (ABOUT 4 CUPS)

1 1/2 POUNDS RUTABAGAS, PEELED, AND CUT INTO 1/2-INCH PIECES (ABOUT 4 CUPS)

2 MEDIUM-SIZED RED ONIONS (ABOUT 1 POUND) PEELED AND CUT INTO 1-INCH-THICK WEDGES

SALT AND FRESHLY GROUND BLACK PEPPER

3 TABLESPOONS BALSAMIC VINEGAR

3 TABLESPOONS CHOPPED FLAT-LEAF PARSLEY

2 TEASPOONS GRATED LEMON ZEST

PARSLEY SPRIGS, FOR GARNISH

SERVES 8 TO 10

1. Position the oven rack in the top third and the other rack in the bottom third of the oven. Preheat the oven to 425 degrees. Spray two rimmed baking sheets or a large roasting pan with nonstick vegetable spray.

2. In a large mixing bowl, whisk together 6 tablespoons of the oil, 2 tablespoons of the thyme, and 2 tablespoons of the marjoram. Add the yams, carrots, parsnips, rutabagas, and onions and toss to coat. Sprinkle the vegetables generously with salt and pepper and divide between the baking sheets, spreading the vegetables evenly.

3. Roast for about 50 minutes, or until tender and brown in spots. Using a spatula, turn the vegetables several times during roasting. Remove from the oven and let the vegetables cool slightly or to room temperature. You can make these up to this point 4 hours ahead of time. If you prefer to serve these warm, you can rewarm them in a 350-degree oven for about 15 minutes, or microwave them on High for about 6 minutes, or until heated through.

4. In a small bowl, whisk the vinegar with the remaining 3 tablespoons of oil, 1 1/2 teaspoons of thyme, and 1 1/2 teaspoons of marjoram. Season to taste with salt and pepper.

5. Transfer the vegetables to a shallow serving dish. Drizzle with the vinaigrette and toss gently. Sprinkle with the chopped parsley and lemon zest. Adjust the seasonings. Garnish with the parsley sprigs. Serve warm or at room temperature.

GINGER-CARROT BISQUE

THIS SOUP IS REALLY NICE AND DELICIOUS. I have it a lot in the fall when there isn't much else around to make—a little ginger gives it a nice flavor. We cook with ginger a lot in our family and we love it. Not a cream soup but puréed, this is easy to make, with good flavor. *mg*

INGREDIENTS

6 TABLESPOONS (3/4 STICK) UNSALTED BUTTER

2 POUNDS CARROTS, PEELED AND THINLY SLICED

2 LARGE ONIONS, FINELY CHOPPED

1 TABLESPOON MINCED PEELED FRESH GINGER

2 TEASPOONS GRATED ORANGE ZEST

1/2 TEASPOON GROUND CORIANDER

5 CUPS HOMEMADE OR CANNED CHICKEN STOCK

1 CUP HALF-AND-HALF

SALT AND FRESHLY GROUND BLACK PEPPER

1/2 CUP MINCED FLAT-LEAF PARSLEY

SERVES 8

1. In a large, heavy saucepan, melt the butter over medium heat. Add the carrots and onions and cook, stirring occasionally, for about 15 minutes, or until the vegetables begin to soften.

2. Add the ginger, orange zest, and coriander and stir to mix. Add 2 cups of the chicken stock and bring to a boil. Reduce the heat to medium-low so that the stock simmers, cover, and cook gently for about 30 minutes, or until the carrots are tender.

3. Transfer the soup to a blender or food processor and purée until smooth. You may have to do this in batches. Return the puréed soup to the pan.

4. Add the remaining 3 cups of stock and the half-and-half to the soup and heat over medium heat until heated through. Season to taste with salt and pepper.

5. Ladle into bowls and sprinkle with parsley. Serve immediately.

Note

This soup does very well prepared a day ahead of time. Let the hot soup cool to room temperature, cover, and refrigerate for up to 24 hours. Reheat over medium heat until hot. Serve garnished with parsley.

TRICOLOR BEET SALAD

BEETS MAY BE THE UNSUNG HERO of the vegetable world. I rarely think of cooking beets—I don't know why—but when I do, I love to make this salad. It's as delicious as it is aesthetically pleasing. *lg*

INGREDIENTS

6 MEDIUM-SIZED BEETS (2 OF EACH OF THREE COLORS, IF AVAILABLE; ABOUT 48 OUNCES BEFORE TRIMMING)

1/3 CUP OLIVE OIL

1/4 CUP BALSAMIC VINEGAR

SALT AND FRESHLY GROUND BLACK PEPPER

PARMESAN OR OTHER HARD CHEESE, FOR SHAVING

1/3 CUP PINE NUTS, TOASTED, SEE NOTE

SERVES 6

1. Preheat the oven to 400 degrees.

2. Clean the beets under cool, running water. Trim the ends and wrap each beet in aluminum foil. Put the foil packets on a baking sheet or shallow tray and bake for 50 minutes to 1 hour, or until fork-tender. Unwrap the beets and let them cool for about 30 minutes, or until cool enough to handle.

3. Slip the skins from the beets; they will slide right off. Slice the beets into thin pieces, about 1/4 inch thick.

4. Arrange the beet slices on a serving platter in a decorative manner with some artistic flair.

5. In a small bowl, whisk together the oil and vinegar. Season to taste with salt and pepper. Drizzle the dressing over the beets.

6. Shave the cheese over the beets to cover lightly. Sprinkle with pine nuts. Serve at room temperature.

Note

To toast pine nuts, spread them in a single layer in a small baking dish or dry skillet. Broil or cook over medium-high heat for 1 to 2 minutes, or until the pine nuts color slightly and are fragrant. Shake the pan and watch carefully so they do not burn.

Gardens

MISSHAPED TOPS OF SMOOTH GREY STONES warmed by the April sun grow bigger as the threadbare bedding of snow, now reduced to sheets, recedes and eventually exposes a blackened composted mattress of seaweed spread in fall. By the next full moon tentative patches of tilled soil are bolstered, prodded, and cajoled to resemble what is proudly called "garden." The backyard plot, a mere pond relative to the slow-rolling sea of blueberry field across the way, shares the same granite islands and dangerous shoals noted on charts of the bay aboard boats that sail here. It's nail-biting work to navigate these waters—the first of many challenges met by the original New England settlers. Today, the toil of everyday life has eased. The long-ago needs of ocean travel and subsistence farming have been reduced, or heightened, to hobbies. What were chores are now choices. Unchanged is the fact that we, both settlers and present residents, have chosen to live here. Hobbies like gardening remind us of the joys and difficulties of our chosen home.

Remains of miles of winding stone walls are monuments to the monumental task of clearing acres of not particularly fertile land in an environment hostile to the growing and harvesting of most everything. It's a short growing season, stretched on both ends. In spring, attempts with hoe and spade are met with belligerence by frozen earth stiff beneath a shallow temperate mud. In fall, it's a race to see who will pick the last cherry tomato before winter claims it: farmer, seagull, deer, neighbor? For who among us has never helped themselves to an apple and justified theft with "Better me than Jack Frost?"

Ah, but in our stunted summer there is great abundance. Even those who do not garden enjoy the shared bounty from neighbors proud of the harvest they have certainly earned. In July there are gifts of the first tomatoes still green and a handful of peas. In August, baskets

of renegade corn and zucchinis the size of small children are abandoned on the doorsteps of anyone who may provide a good home. We "put up," jarring and canning and freezing all that exceeds what can be eaten fresh, for soon the seaweed will be dragged from the shore and the garden put to bed. *lg*

COOL GREEN SALAD

I COLLECT COOKBOOKS AND COOKING MAGAZINES. Because I am totally addicted and can't bear to throw them out, I have a cluttered house to say the least. A few years ago, I remember an article about a Washington, D.C., dinner party. The menu caught my eye because evidently Senator Bill Cohen from Maine brought a dish called Cool Green Salad. I love Senator Cohen (who doesn't?), so perhaps that had something to do with why I made the salad for my next dinner party. I've been making it ever since. *mg*

DRESSING

1/2 CUP EXTRA-VIRGIN OLIVE OIL

1/4 CUP RED WINE VINEGAR

1 TABLESPOON SNIPPED PARSLEY

1 TEASPOON DRY MUSTARD

1 TEASPOON SALT

1 GARLIC CLOVE, CUT IN HALF

FRESHLY GROUND BLACK PEPPER

SALAD

1 LARGE HEAD RED- OR GREEN-LEAF LETTUCE, TORN INTO BITE-SIZED PIECES (ABOUT 5 CUPS)

1 POUND SPINACH, TORN INTO BITE-SIZED PIECES (ABOUT 5 CUPS)

1 BUNCH WATERCRESS, STEMS REMOVED

1 LARGE SEEDLESS ENGLISH CUCUMBER, SLICED

1 MEDIUM ONION, THINLY SLICED INTO RINGS

SERVES 10

1. In a jar with a tight-fitting lid or a similar container, combine the oil, vinegar, parsley, mustard, salt, garlic, and pepper to taste. Cover and shake well. Refrigerate for at least 1 hour or until chilled. The dressing will keep in the refrigerator for up to a week.

2. In a large salad bowl, toss together the lettuce, spinach, watercress, cucumber, and onion slices. Remove the garlic and drizzle with the chilled dressing. Toss again to mix and serve immediately.

MAMA'S COLESLAW

MY MOUTH STILL WATERS when I recall the coleslaw my mother made every Saturday night to go with our baked beans and hot biscuits. This was before food processors and so I was often left with the job of shredding the cabbage and carrots. Today, I usually use the food processor but am not shy about using a knife or box grater instead. *mg*

INGREDIENTS

ONE 2- TO 2 1/2-POUND GREEN CABBAGE HEAD, SHREDDED

2 LARGE CARROTS, SHREDDED

2 CUPS MAYONNAISE

1/2 CUP SOUR CREAM

1 TEASPOON CELERY SEED

1 TEASPOON MUSTARD SEED

1 TEASPOON SUGAR

SALT

SERVES 6 TO 8

1. In a large bowl, toss together the cabbage and carrots.
2. In another bowl, stir together the mayonnaise, sour cream, celery seed, mustard seed, and sugar. Season to taste with salt.
3. Toss the cabbage with the dressing. Cover and chill for at least 2 hours before serving.

LINDA & MARTHA GREENLAW

GINGERED FRUIT SLAW

AT FIRST GLANCE, THE INGREDIENTS LIST for this will seem long but once you decide to make it, you won't be disappointed. We love it. I make coleslaw a lot in the summer and this one is a favorite on picnics because it travels well and has no mayonnaise. *mg*

INGREDIENTS

TWO 8-OUNCE CANS PINEAPPLE CHUNKS OR TIDIBTS

6 OUNCES (ABOUT 1 CUP) MIXED DRIED FRUIT, COARSELY CHOPPED

2 LARGE CARROTS, SHREDDED

1 SMALL HEAD GREEN CABBAGE, SHREDDED (5 OR 6 CUPS)

1/2 CUP CHOPPED WALNUTS

2 TABLESPOONS VEGETABLE OIL

2 TABLESPOONS HONEY

1 TABLESPOON FRESH LEMON JUICE

1/2 TEASPOON GROUND GINGER

SALT AND FRESHLY GROUND BLACK PEPPER

SERVES 4 TO 6

1. Drain the pineapple. Reserve 1/3 cup of the juice. Cut the chunks, if using, into small 1/4-inch pieces.

2. In a 3-quart, rigid plastic lidded container, layer the pineapple bits, fruit pieces, and carrots. Top with a layer of cabbage and walnuts.

3. In a jar with a tight-fitting lid or a similar container, combine the oil, honey, lemon juice, ginger, and reserved pineapple juice. Cover tightly and shake well.

4. Pour the dressing over the salad without stirring. Cover the slaw and refrigerate for several hours or overnight.

5. Just before serving, toss well. Season to taste with salt and pepper.

Note

Layering the cabbage and walnuts on top of the slaw keeps them crisper as it chills.

CLARA'S MINTED GREEN PEA SALAD

CLARA STUPINSKI AND I USED TO PLAY RACQUETBALL five days a week when the kids were younger and before I moved to the island for good. She almost always beat me but I loved her in spite of it! On special occasions, the club had covered dish luncheons, and we could always count on Clara to bring this minted pea salad—especially delicious when the fresh mint ran rampant in summer gardens. *mg*

INGREDIENTS

ONE 10-OUNCE PACKAGE FROZEN PEAS

3 TABLESPOONS MAYONNAISE

1 TEASPOON LEMON JUICE

1 TEASPOON CHOPPED FRESH MINT OR 1/4 TEASPOON DRIED MINT

1/2 TEASPOON SUGAR

1/8 TEASPOON SALT

1/2 CUP CHOPPED CELERY (2 RIBS CELERY)

8 BOSTON LETTUCE LEAVES

LEMON SLICES, FOR GARNISH

MINT LEAVES, FOR GARNISH

SERVES 4

1. Put the peas in a colander and thaw under running water. Set aside to drain.
2. In a mixing bowl, whisk together the mayonnaise, lemon juice, mint, sugar, and salt.
3. Add the drained peas and celery and stir to mix with the mayonaise.
4. Lay the lettuce leaves on a serving platter in an overlapping pattern. Spoon the pea salad on the lettuce. Garnish with lemon slices and mint leaves. Chill before serving.

PEAS AND TURNIPS WITH DILL BUTTER

I USE DILL BUTTER TO FLAVOR FISH AND VEGETABLES so often I guess you could call it one of my

culinary signatures. I grow fresh dill in a window box outside the side door, away from the ocean, where I can see it from the dining area window. I also grow boxes of parsley, tarragon, thyme, basil, and rosemary in this protected place and it's not unusual for me to get inspiration for a dish just by gazing at the profusion of herbs. I can't have much of a garden on the island because of the deer, so I have become very content with the herbs. Herb-growing season was long over when I made this dish up one year for Thanksgiving, but I managed to get fresh dill in the market. Everyone decided they liked this as much as the more traditional mashed turnips I usually make. *mg*

INGREDIENTS

8 TABLESPOONS (1 STICK) UNSALTED BUTTER, AT ROOM TEMPERATURE

4 TABLESPOONS CHOPPED FRESH DILL

SALT AND FRESHLY GROUND BLACK PEPPER

8 BACON SLICES, CRUMBLED (OPTIONAL)

1 1/4 POUNDS TURNIPS, PEELED AND CUT INTO 1/2-INCH CUBES (ABOUT 4 CUPS) (SEE NOTE)

1 TEASPOON SUGAR (OPTIONAL)

TWO 16-OUNCE BAGS FROZEN PETITE PEAS, THAWED

SERVES 8 TO 10

1. In a small bowl, mix together 6 tablespoons of the butter and 3 tablespoons of the dill to blend. Season to taste with salt and pepper. (The dill butter may be made 2 days ahead if covered and refrigerated.)

2. In a skillet, sauté the bacon, if using, over medium heat until brown and crisp. Using a slotted spoon, transfer to paper towels to drain. Let the bacon cool to room temperature.

3. In a large nonstick skillet, melt the remaining 2 tablespoons of butter over medium-high heat. Add the turnips and sauté for about 9 minutes, or until tender and golden. If you find the turnips taste sharp, add a little sugar.

4. Add the peas and dill butter and cook, stirring, for about 3 minutes, or until the peas are heated through and the butter melts.

5. Stir in the bacon, if using. Season to taste with salt and pepper. Transfer to a bowl, garnish with the remaining tablespoon of dill, and serve.

— *Note* —

Turnips are available in the freezer section packaged in 1 1/4-pound bags and cut into 1/2-inch cubes. If you prefer, use these instead of fresh.

PIQUANT GREEN BEANS

IF I CAN'T GET FRESH GREEN BEANS, I don't cook them. Luckily, I can usually find them in the markets and even at the little store on the island. My family loves them, and this preparation is a nice change from the usual steamed and buttered beans. *mg*

INGREDIENTS

1 1/2 POUNDS FRESH GREEN BEANS, TRIMMED

3 BACON SLICES, CHOPPED

2 TABLESPOONS DICED PIMIENTO

2 TABLESPOONS RED WINE VINEGAR

1 TABLESPOON WORCESTERSHIRE SAUCE

1/4 TEASPOON SUGAR

1/4 TEASPOON DRY MUSTARD

2 DROPS RED PEPPER SAUCE, SUCH AS TABASCO

SERVES 6

1. In a steaming basket set over boiling water, steam the beans, tightly covered, for about 15 minutes, or until tender. Drain and transfer to a bowl.
2. In a skillet, sauté the bacon over medium heat until brown and crisp. Using a slotted spoon, transfer to paper towels to drain. Add to the beans.
3. To the bacon drippings in the skillet, add the pimiento, vinegar, Worcestershire sauce, sugar, mustard, and red pepper sauce. Bring to a boil, stirring constantly, for about 1 minute until blended. Pour over the beans, mix well, and serve.

STUFFED TOMATOES

THIS IS MY FAVORITE WAY to stuff tomatoes. It's especially good during the short time at the end of the summer when our Maine gardens are bursting with ripe tomatoes. I urge you to try it with garden-fresh tomatoes. The sausage makes it robust, more of a simple main course than a side dish. You will love it. It easily serves 6 as a light main course or more as a side dish. *mg*

INGREDIENTS

6 MEDIUM-SIZED FIRM, RIPE TOMATOES (ABOUT 3 POUNDS), STEMMED

SALT AND FRESHLY GROUND BLACK PEPPER

4 SWEET OR HOT ITALIAN SAUSAGE LINKS (ABOUT 1/2 POUND)

1 TABLESPOON OLIVE OIL

1/2 CUP FINELY CHOPPED ONION

1 GARLIC CLOVE, FINELY MINCED

1 1/2 CUPS COOKED LONG-GRAIN RICE

3 TABLESPOONS PINE NUTS

2 TABLESPOONS FINELY CHOPPED PARSLEY

1 TABLESPOON FINELY CHOPPED BASIL

1/4 CUP GRATED PARMESAN CHEESE

1 LARGE EGG, SLIGHTLY BEATEN

SERVES 6 TO 12

1. Preheat the oven to 375 degrees. Lightly oil a baking dish large enough to hold the tomato halves in a single layer. You may need two dishes.

2. Split the tomatoes in half and gently squeeze each tomato half over a bowl so that the seeds, juice, and pulp fall into it; reserve. Sprinkle each tomato half with salt and pepper to taste and set aside.

3. Remove the sausage meat from the casing. In a skillet, heat the oil, add the onion and garlic, and cook over medium heat for about 2 minutes, just until very slightly softened.

4. Raise the heat to medium-high and add the sausage meat, breaking it up with the side of a heavy kitchen spoon or wooden spoon, and cook for 4 to 5 minutes, or until the meat changes color. Add the reserved tomato seeds, juice, and pulp and cook for about 5 minutes, or until the liquid evaporates. Remove the skillet from the heat to cool slightly.

5. With the skillet off the heat, stir in the rice, pine nuts, parsley, basil, and half the cheese. Add the egg, stir well, and then season to taste with salt and pepper. Let cool.

6. Arrange the tomato halves, cut sides up, in the baking dish. Spoon the filling into the indentations and over the tops of the tomato halves, piling and rounding with your fingers. Sprinkle with the remaining cheese. Bake 30 minutes. Serve hot or at room temperature.

FRESH LEMON RICE

NOWADAYS I TEND TO USE BROWN RICE for every rice dish because it's "heart smart," but I still prefer the way white rice looks. I make this to accompany baked haddock or a similar white fish. The lemon flavor nicely complements the fish. *mg*

INGREDIENTS

4 TABLESPOONS (1/2 STICK) UNSALTED BUTTER

2 1/2 CUPS LONG-GRAIN RICE

4 1/2 CUPS CHICKEN STOCK

1/2 CUP DRY WHITE VERMOUTH

1 1/2 TEASPOONS SALT

PINCH OF WHITE PEPPER

GRATED ZEST OF 2 LEMONS

1/4 CUP MINCED FLAT-LEAF PARSLEY

SERVES 8 TO 10; MAKES 8 CUPS

1. In a large skillet, melt the butter over medium heat. Add the rice and stir for about 2 minutes, or until the grains are well coated with butter. Add the stock, vermouth, salt, and pepper.

2. Bring to the boil over medium-high heat. Reduce the heat to low so the liquid simmers. Cover tightly and cook for about 20 minutes, or until the liquid is absorbed.

3. Remove the rice from the heat and stir in the lemon zest and parsley. Serve immediately.

MAKE-AHEAD PARTY POTATOES

IF I WANT TO MAKE A HIT with the men at my dinner table, I serve this potato dish. Everyone  loves it, but men seem to be special fans. I'm a big fan, too, but for different reasons. I love the way it tastes, but I also love that it's made ahead of time and then only needs to be popped in the oven for about 40 minutes before serving. *mg*

INGREDIENTS

6 MEDIUM-SIZED POTATOES (ABOUT 4 POUNDS), PEELED AND QUARTERED

8 TABLESPOONS (1 STICK) UNSALTED BUTTER

8 OUNCES CREAM CHEESE, CUT INTO SMALL PIECES, AT ROOM TEMPERATURE

1 CUP SOUR CREAM

2 TEASPOONS SALT

1/4 TEASPOON FRESHLY GRATED BLACK PEPPER

1/4 TEASPOON PAPRIKA

DASH OF CUMIN

SERVES 10 TO 12

1. Put the potatoes in a pot and add enough water to cover by an inch or two. Bring to a boil over medium-high heat, reduce the heat, and simmer for about 20 minutes, or until fork-tender. Drain and set aside.

2. Put the same pot back on the heat and melt the butter. Add the cream cheese and whisk until the mixture is smooth.

3. Force the potatoes through a ricer or food mill into the pot and mix with the butter-cream cheese mixture. Add the sour cream, salt, and pepper and stir until smooth.

4. Spread the potatoes evenly in a 9 by 13-inch baking dish and sprinkle with the paprika and cumin. Let the potatoes cool slightly, then cover with plastic wrap. Refrigerate until ready to cook. These will keep well overnight.

5. Preheat the oven to 350 degrees. Remove the potatoes from the refrigerator about 15 minutes before baking.

6. Bake the potatoes, uncovered, for 35 to 45 minutes, or until heated through and a slight crust forms on top. Serve immediately.

PEAS WITH MINT

THIS IS A LITTLE DRESSIER THAN other pea dishes and if you're having company, it works well as the green dish on the table. Fresh mint is easy to come by and most of us have a bottle of Grand Marnier kicking around. *mg*

INGREDIENTS

THREE 10-OUNCE PACKAGES FROZEN PEAS, PARTIALLY THAWED

1 TEASPOON SUGAR

TWO 8-OUNCE CANS WATER CHESTNUTS, DRAINED, SLICED, AND CHOPPED, IF LARGE

5 TABLESPOONS UNSALTED BUTTER

1/4 CUP GRAND MARNIER

1 1/4 TABLESPOONS CHOPPED FRESH MINT LEAVES

1 TEASPOON SALT

SERVES 8 TO 10

1. In a large saucepan, bring 1 cup of water to a boil. Add the peas and sugar, let the liquid return to a simmer, and cook for 5 minutes, or until the peas are hot. Drain the peas and transfer to a serving bowl.

2. Add the water chestnuts, butter, Grand Marnier, mint leaves, and salt. Toss gently and thoroughly. Serve.

FLUFFY TWICE-BAKED POTATOES

ALTHOUGH I HAD OFTEN ASSISTED my mother in the kitchen as she prepared for one of her exquisite dinner parties (usually peeling, chopping, and stirring under her very particular eye), the first time that I was fully and solely responsible for actually feeding anyone other than the family dog was when I became employed as the "cookie" aboard a commercial fishing boat. In need of money for college, I sort of lied about my experience to land the job, and being the only female on board with a crew of six hungry fishermen, I wished my mother had allowed me more of a role in the process.

"Meat and potatoes—and plenty of 'em" was all I was told about what might be appreciated and expected for thirty consecutive dinners while at sea. I had absolutely no idea what to do with the various hunks of frozen cuts of meat, with which I was most unfamiliar. But potatoes I could handle. I had been taught at the tender age of eight how to select, bake, scoop out the hot flesh, mix it with butter, sour cream, and cumin, stuff it back into the skin, and reheat before serving. I remember being quite proud of these fluffy twice-bakes when presenting them to the crew and also recall my embarrassment and humiliation when one man sarcastically called them "elegant." *lg*

INGREDIENTS

4 BAKING POTATOES (ABOUT 2 POUNDS TOTAL), SCRUBBED CLEAN

1/2 CUP SOUR CREAM

3/4 CUP MILK

1/2 TEASPOON SALT

1/2 TEASPOON GROUND CUMIN

DASH OF FRESHLY GROUND BLACK PEPPER

2 TABLESPOONS (1/4 STICK) UNSALTED BUTTER

PAPRIKA

2 BACON SLICES (OPTIONAL)

SERVES 4

1. Preheat the oven to 425 degrees.

2. Prick the potatoes with a fork in several places and bake on the oven rack for 50 to 60 minutes, or until fork-tender. Remove from the oven and let cool until cool enough to handle. Do not turn off the oven but reduce the temperature to 375 degrees.

3. Meanwhile, in the bowl of an electric mixer set on medium speed and fitted with the paddle attachment, blend the sour cream, milk, salt, cumin, and pepper. Set aside for 10 minutes.

4. Cut a thin slice, about 1/2 inch thick, off the top quarter of the wide side of each potato. Discard the slices and scoop out the centers of the potatoes, leaving a 1/4- to 1/2-inch-thick shell of potato and jacket. Put the scooped-out potatoes and the butter in the bowl with the sour cream mixture.

5. With the mixer set on medium speed, beat until fluffy, adding more milk, if necessary. Spoon this back into the potato shells. Sprinkle the tops with paprika. Set the filled potatoes in a baking dish large enough to hold them without crowding.

6. Bake for 25 minutes, or until heated through.

7. In a skillet, cook the bacon, if using, until crispy. Drain on paper towels. When cool, break the bacon into pieces.

8. To serve, top the potatoes with the bacon pieces, if desired.

BECKY TALBOT'S MUSTARD ONIONS

ALTHOUGH I'VE NEVER MET BECKY TALBOT, I feel as though I know her because I have been making her mustard onions for years and years. She must be quite a gal. Not only is she a good cook, she's my friend Ginny Brehmer's sister. *mg*

INGREDIENTS

2 TABLESPOONS (1/4 STICK) UNSALTED BUTTER

3 TABLESPOONS ALL-PURPOSE FLOUR

1 CUP HOMEMADE OR CANNED CHICKEN STOCK, HEATED

3 TABLESPOONS YELLOW MUSTARD

2 1/2 TABLESPOONS PACKED LIGHT BROWN SUGAR

1 1/2 TABLESPOONS GRANULATED SUGAR

1 TEASPOON WORCESTERSHIRE SAUCE

2 POUNDS PEARL ONIONS, PEELED, OR TWO 16-OUNCE BAGS
PEELED FROZEN PEARL ONIONS, THAWED TO ROOM TEMPERATURE

SALT AND FRESHLY GROUND BLACK PEPPER

SERVES 6

1. In a large skillet, heat the butter over medium heat until foaming. Sprinkle the flour over the butter and cook for 2 to 3 minutes, stirring with a wooden spoon or spatula, until the flour and butter form a smooth roux and the flour loses its raw flavor.

2. Add the stock, mustard, brown sugar, granulated sugar, and Worcestershire sauce to the pan and stir gently over medium heat for about 5 minutes, or until the sauce is smooth and blended.

3. If using fresh pearl onions, cook them in lightly salted boiling water for 8 to 10 minutes, or until fork-tender. Drain. If using frozen onions, make sure they are at room temperature.

4. Add the onions to the pan and simmer gently over medium-low heat for 10 to 12 minutes, or until the onions are tender and heated through. Season to taste with salt and pepper. Serve immediately.

GLAZED BITTERSWEET ONIONS

THESE ARE SIMPLY THE BEST! Glazed bittersweet onions are a staple of the Greenlaws' Thanksgiving Day feast. One problem: no leftovers. *lg*

INGREDIENTS

ONE 10- TO 12-OUNCE CAN CONDENSED BEEF CONSOMMÉ

2 POUNDS PEARL ONIONS, PEELED, OR TWO 16-OUNCE BAGS PEELED FROZEN PEARL ONIONS, THAWED

1/4 CUP UNSALTED BUTTER OR MARGARINE, SOFTENED

1/3 CUP SUGAR

4 TEASPOONS FRESH LEMON JUICE

1/4 TEASPOON SALT, OR TO TASTE

FEW DASHES OF WHITE PEPPER

SERVES 6

1. Pour the consommé into a large saucepan. Fill the can with water and add to the pan. Add the onions and bring to a boil over medium-high heat. Reduce the heat to medium and simmer for about 15 minutes, or until the onions are tender when pierced with a fork or skewer.

2. Remove from the heat, cover the pan, and set aside to cool.

3. Drain the onions, reserving the stock for another use. Pat the onions dry.

4. In a large, heavy skillet, heat the butter and sugar over medium-low heat for about 1 minute, stirring constantly with a long-handled wooden spoon, until caramel colored.

5. Remove the skillet from the heat and immediately stir in the lemon juice (be careful; it will splatter). Add the onions, stirring until coated with the caramel. Break up any bits of caramelized sugar.

6. Return the skillet to the heat and simmer over medium-low heat, shaking the pan occasionally, for about 30 minutes, or until the onions turn a beautiful copper color. Season with salt and pepper. If you want a thicker sauce, remove the onions with a slotted spoon and cook the sauce over medium-high heat until syrupy.

CHAPTER 8

BISCUITS AND
OTHER BREADS

MOLASSES CORNBREAD

A COUPLE OF YEARS AGO, I had dinner with my cousin John and his partner Rick at their home in southern Maine. Rick, a wonderful cook, had prepared a big pot of chili and some cornbread that he baked in a cast-iron skillet. When he pulled the skillet from the oven, the bread was so brown that I assumed he had scorched it and couldn't believe it when he brought it to the table. Closer inspection and questions revealed that the dark color was from molasses. It was yummy and perfect with the chili. I have called Rick on several occasions to get the recipe and yet can never seem to find it every time I want to prepare it. To call again would be embarrassing, so I'm winging this one. *lg*

INGREDIENTS

2 CUPS ALL-PURPOSE FLOUR

1 1/3 CUPS YELLOW OR WHITE CORNMEAL

1/3 CUP SUGAR

3 TEASPOONS BAKING POWDER

3/4 TEASPOON SALT

2 LARGE EGGS

3/4 CUP DARK MOLASSES

1/3 CUP VEGETABLE OIL

1 1/2 CUPS MILK

SERVES 8 TO 10

1. Preheat the oven to 400 degrees. Butter a 9 by 13-inch baking pan.

2. In a mixing bowl, whisk together the flour, cornmeal, sugar, baking powder, and salt.

3. Add the eggs, molasses, and oil and stir with a wooden spoon or fork until blended. Slowly add the milk and stir until the batter is smooth.

4. Transfer the batter to the pan and spread it evenly. Bake for 20 to 25 minutes, or until lightly browned and a toothpick inserted in the center of the cornbread comes out clean.

5. Let the cornbread cool in the pan set on a wire rack. Cut into squares and serve warm or at room temperature.

RED PEPPER AND CHEDDAR CORNBREAD

THIS EXTRA-MOIST BREAD IS GREAT with soup or chili. It looks good and is a really simple recipe that you can throw together at the last minute. It's not spicy but has a nice little zip. *mg*

INGREDIENTS

ONE 8 1/2-OUNCE PACKAGE CORN MUFFIN MIX

ONE 7-OUNCE JAR ROASTED RED PEPPERS, DRAINED AND CHOPPED

4 OUNCES COARSELY SHREDDED CHEDDAR CHEESE (1 CUP)

PINCH OF CAYENNE PEPPER

SERVES 6 TO 8

1. Preheat the oven to 400 degrees. Grease an 8-inch-square baking dish.
2. Prepare the batter according to package directions for corn bread. Stir in the chopped peppers, cheese, and cayenne pepper.
3. Transfer the batter to the pan and spread it evenly in the pan. Bake for 20 to 25 minutes, or until lightly browned and a toothpick inserted in the center of the cornbread comes out clean.
4. Let the cornbread cool in the pan set on a wire rack. Cut into squares and serve warm or at room temperature.

Note

You can make cornbread from scratch and add the peppers, cheese, and cayenne, if you prefer.

GRACIE'S MAKE-AHEAD BAKED FRENCH TOAST

WHEN WE WERE BUILDING OUR COTTAGE on Isle au Haut, we spent a great deal of time at my sister Gracie's house. My kids just loved staying with their Aunt Gracie and Uncle Bud, and why wouldn't they? Gracie was in the habit of rising early and putting French toast in the oven so that it was ready when they piled out of bed on a bright summer morning and arrived at the breakfast table. It's a great recipe because the French toast is prepared well ahead of time—even the night before—and so having it ready when the household wakes up is not as much of a sacrifice as it may sound. *mg*

INGREDIENTS

4 LARGE EGGS

1/2 CUP LIGHT CREAM

1/2 CUP MILK

1 TABLESPOON HONEY

1 TEASPOON PURE VANILLA EXTRACT

1/4 TEASPOON GROUND NUTMEG

8 SLICES DAY-OLD BREAD, CUT 1 INCH THICK (I PREFER FRENCH BREAD)

6 TABLESPOONS (3/4 STICK) UNSALTED BUTTER, MELTED

MAPLE SYRUP, GENTLY WARMED

SERVES 4

1. In the bowl of a food processor fitted with the metal blade, combine the eggs, cream, milk, honey, vanilla, and nutmeg. Process until smooth. Alternatively, mix this by hand with a wire whisk.

2. Arrange the bread slices in a snug layer in a shallow, freezer-safe dish just large enough to hold them.

3. Pour the batter over the bread and let it sit a few minutes to soak in. Gently turn the slices over and let them soak up the rest of the batter.

4. Put the dish in the freezer, uncovered, for at least 4 hours or overnight, until frozen. (Once it is frozen, the bread slices can be packed in an airtight container or plastic freezer bag for up to 2 weeks.)

5. Preheat the oven to 375 degrees. Lightly butter a baking sheet.

6. Put the frozen bread on the baking sheet. Brush each slice on one side with half the melted butter. Bake for about 10 to 15 minutes, then turn over and cook for another 15 minutes. Turn the bread slices over and brush with the remaining butter. Bake for about 8 minutes longer, or until nicely browned.

7. Serve the French toast immediately with warm maple syrup on the side.

GRAMMIE MAD'S YORKSHIRE PUDDING

SOME OF THE KIDS affectionately call Jim's mother, Mattie, Grammie Mad. She taught me to make Yorkshire pudding the old-fashioned way with pan drippings from a roast beef and right in the pan with the meat. I don't make it in the pan anymore, although my daughter Rhonda, who lives in Harpswell, Maine, does because her kids love it. Her daughter Mattie is my granddaughter and whenever she comes home from college her mother makes Yorkshire pudding for her. *mg*

INGREDIENTS

6 TABLESPOONS BEEF FAT FROM A ROAST BEEF OR
6 TABLESPOONS (3/4 STICK) UNSALTED BUTTER,
MELTED (SEE NOTE)

4 TABLESPOONS SIFTED ALL-PURPOSE FLOUR

1 LARGE EGG, BEATEN

1/2 TEASPOON SALT

1 CUP MILK

SERVES 6 TO 8

1. Preheat the oven to 425 degrees. Put the fat in a 9-inch pie plate or oven-safe skillet.

2. Put 2 tablespoons of the sifted flour into a mixing bowl. Add the beaten egg and mix well with a fork. Add the remaining 2 tablespoons of flour, the salt, and the milk. Beat well with a fork, whisk, or egg beater.

3. Meanwhile, bring the fat to a sizzle over high heat or in the oven. Pour the batter into the hot fat and immediately transfer to the oven. Bake for 45 to 50 minutes, or until the pudding is puffed and golden brown. Serve immediately.

Note

Yorkshire pudding was traditionally baked in the roasting pan with the roast, but I always bake it separately, as I suspect most people do. It's best made with the pan drippings from the roast, but you can use butter if need be. Just make sure the fat is sizzling hot when you pour the batter over it.

BAKING POWDER BISCUITS

IN MY OPINION, biscuits are one of life's little mysteries. Both my sister Gracie and I make them all the time and we both learned how from our mother. Gracie's are high and flaky and just about melt in your mouth. Mine, on the other hand, taste just as good but you wouldn't want to enter them in a biscuit-making contest! For light, fluffy biscuits, use a light hand when mixing the dough. *mg*

INGREDIENTS

2 CUPS ALL-PURPOSE FLOUR

1 TABLESPOON BAKING POWDER

1 TEASPOON SALT

4 HEAPING TABLESPOONS SOLID VEGETABLE SHORTENING,
SUCH AS CRISCO, OR UNSALTED BUTTER

3/4 CUP MILK

MAKES 16 TO 20 BISCUITS

1. Preheat the oven to 425 degrees.

2. In a mixing bowl, sift together the flour, baking powder, and salt.

3. Add the shortening and using a fork, pastry blender, or your fingers, mix the fat into the flour until the mixture resembles coarse crumbs. This should take about 1 minute. You can do this in a food processor fitted with a medium blade. Pulse 4 to 5 times.

4. Add the milk, a little at a time, stirring lightly after each addition.

5. Turn out onto a lightly floured work surface and pat into a round shape. Using a rolling pin, roll into a round about 1/2 inch thick. Do not press on the dough but roll out from the center with quick, light strokes.

6. With a 2 1/2- to 3-inch-round biscuit cutter or overturned glass, cut out as many biscuits as you can and lay them on an ungreased baking sheet. Gather the remaining dough and roll it out again. Cut out more biscuits. Handle the dough gently as you work with it.

7. Bake the biscuits for 10 to 12 minutes, or until golden brown.

Wintry Sundays

WINTRY SUNDAYS ARE THE BEST FOR GUILT-FREE NONPRODUCTION. On cold, snowy Sunday mornings, I sometimes allow myself to stay in bed until after 7:00 A.M. I don't fidget or obsess that I am not "doing anything" if I spend a Sunday writing letters, doing laundry, and preparing a very involved recipe for a special Sunday dinner. I am sure the relaxed Sunday attitude stems from a childhood (and I may be dating myself here) when all places of commercial business were closed on the first day of every week—even gas stations.

The very best of wintry Sundays were at an age when I was still young enough to wear a "snorkel jacket," yet old enough to leave it in the bleachers while skating around the hockey arena at Bowdoin College in shirtsleeves. We never attended church, but a Greenlaw Sunday was ritualistic in many ways. My father's parents, Gram and Gramp, came to dinner. Gramp beat me at ping-pong in the basement, and my siblings and I all skated at the college from 3:00 P.M. to 5:00 P.M. when the rink was open to the public.

The price of admission for two hours of skating was two dollars, and I remember clearly Dad handing me a five with permission to buy hot cocoa at the concession stand with some of the change. Although two sisters and a brother skated every Sunday too, and I may have helped lace the twins' skates up, once the gate opened at three o'clock sharp, I hit the ice unconnected to anyone, with the most incredible liberating feeling of independence. For two hours I would revel in this feeling, lost in thought among perhaps one hundred other skaters doing the same thing. We started out clockwise, around and around, faster and faster, until the bleachers and boards were just a blur. With three bucks in the pocket of my dungarees, I felt pretty important skating on the exact same ice as the players on the Polar Bears' hockey team. The bleacher blur was to the left until the monitor blew his whistle to reverse direction. The crowd of lone skaters stopped with a crisp, synchronized spray of fine snow of blades across ice and began again, counterclockwise, faster and faster, the blur on the right.

At halftime, two shrill blasts of the whistle pierced music and thought, signaling skaters to leave the rink through gates to the stands while the old man on the big machine cleaned the ice. The machine was so slow and the line at the concession stand was so long. I would nervously pivot my attention back and forth between the machine's progress and the head of the line, where I would eventually order hot chocolate and hobble hurriedly on skated feet back to a seat closest to the gate. The air was cold and still but for the steam rising from under the machine and over the cup of cocoa. No matter how long I waited to take the first sip, I burned my tongue, bad—scorched. There was no time for cooling the sweet chocolate drink. Timing was critical. The goal—and I always achieved it—was to finish the cocoa just as the old man on the machine exited the rink and bolt through the gate with the speed of a player ending time in the penalty box onto the ice now like glass.

Five o'clock came quickly. I would happily become a member of my family again. As we piled into the waiting car, someone always broke the silence by remarking that it was dark. Eight fatigued ankles and four burned tongues would enjoy ice cream sundaes after baths, and before sleep filled with anticipation of the next Sunday. I eventually outgrew the skates and the burned tongues, but never the good feelings of a do-nothing wintry Sunday. *lg*

OLD-FASHIONED STEAMED BROWN BREAD

USUALLY MAMA BAKED BISCUITS to go with our Saturday night baked beans, but sometimes, as a change of pace, she'd get out the big kettle and make a moist and tender steamed brown bread. This was the preferred accompaniment for baked beans for generations of New Englanders, so it felt nice to be carrying on that tradition. And besides, it's absolutely delicious! *mg*

INGREDIENTS

1/2 CUP YELLOW CORNMEAL

1/2 CUP RYE FLOUR (SEE NOTE)

1/2 CUP WHOLE WHEAT FLOUR (SEE NOTE)

1 TEASPOON BAKING SODA

1/2 TEASPOON SALT

1 CUP BUTTERMILK OR SOUR MILK (SEE NOTE)

1/3 CUP DARK MOLASSES

1/2 CUP DARK RAISINS (OPTIONAL)

SERVES 6 TO 8

1. Grease a clean and dry 13- to 14-ounce coffee can.

2. In a large bowl, whisk together the cornmeal, rye flour, whole wheat flour, baking soda, and salt. Make a well in the center, add the buttermilk or sour milk and molasses, and whisk until well blended. Stir in the raisins, if using.

3. Pour batter into the greased mold and cover tightly with aluminum foil. Place the coffee can, foil-covered side up, in a deep pot with a lid and pour in enough boiling water to come halfway up the can.

4. Cover the pot and steam over low heat for about 1 1/2 hours, or until a skewer inserted in the center of the bread comes out clean. Lift the can out using oven mitts and cool on a rack. Tap the bread out of the can (or, if necessary, remove the bottom with a can opener and push the bread out). Serve warm or at room temperature. The bread can be reheated in the steamer or in a microwave.

Notes

A good place to buy these specialty flours is a health food store, where they're sold in bulk. They are also available in many supermarkets. Neither rye nor whole wheat flour keep as long as all-purpose flour. Store in the refrigerator and use within 3 or 4 months.

To sour milk, add 2 teaspoons of white vinegar to 1 cup of milk and let stand for 10 minutes.

CHAPTER 9
PLAIN OLD-FASHIONED SWEETS

NANA'S POUND CAKE

NANA'S POUND CAKE, a mainstay of the Palmer-Blaisdell family, has been passed down on the island. The recipe belongs to Nana Kitty, also known as Katherine Palmer of Newport, Rhode Island, who bequeathed it to her children, grandchildren, and great-grandchildren. No wonder it shows up at any number of local events! And everyone who bakes it fondly remembers Nana Kitty with every serving of this indulgent cake. The icing is not necessary, but it dresses the cake up a little. *mg*

CAKE

1 2/3 CUPS GRANULATED SUGAR

1 CUP (2 STICKS) UNSALTED BUTTER OR MARGARINE, SOFTENED

5 LARGE EGGS

2 TEASPOONS PURE VANILLA EXTRACT OR 1 TABLESPOON BRANDY

2 CUPS ALL-PURPOSE FLOUR

PINCH OF SALT

ICING

1 CUP SIFTED CONFECTIONERS' SUGAR

1 TABLESPOON MILK OR ORANGE JUICE

1/4 TEASPOON PURE VANILLA EXTRACT

SERVES 8 TO 10

1. Preheat the oven to 350 degrees. Lightly butter a 10- or 12-cup tube or Bundt pan, or a 9 by 5-inch loaf pan.
2. In the bowl of an electric mixer fitted with the paddle attachment and set at medium speed, cream the sugar and butter for 4 to 5 minutes, or until light and fluffy. Add the eggs, one at a time, beating well after each addition. Beat in the vanilla.
3. Reduce the speed to low and gradually add the flour and salt. When well incorporated, scrape the batter into the pan. Bake for 50 to 55 minutes, or until lightly browned and a toothpick inserted in the center of the cake comes out clean.
4. Let the cake cool in the pan for about 10 minutes. Gently loosen it from the sides of the pan with a kitchen knife and then invert on a wire rack to cool completely.
5. In a small bowl, whisk together the confectioners' sugar, milk or juice, and vanilla.
6. Set the cake on a plate or tray and insert some wax paper strips under it to catch the dripping icing. Using a spoon, drizzle the icing over the cake. Remove the wax paper before serving.

TERRY'S SOUR CREAM RHUBARB SQUARES

I HAVE SHARED THIS RECIPE with many friends, who in turn share it with their family and friends. It's just so good it makes its own welcome in every kitchen. When the twins, Chuck and Biffy, were young, Terry was a neighbor with children about the same age. Not only did we take the kids with us everywhere we went, Terry shared her rhubarb patch with me—and her recipes. *mg*

INGREDIENTS

1/2 CUP SUGAR

1/2 CUP CHOPPED WALNUTS OR PECANS

1 TABLESPOON UNSALTED BUTTER OR MARGARINE, MELTED

1 TEASPOON GROUND CINNAMON

1 1/2 CUPS PACKED LIGHT BROWN SUGAR

1/2 CUP SOLID VEGETABLE SHORTENING

1 LARGE EGG

2 CUPS ALL-PURPOSE FLOUR

1 TEASPOON BAKING SODA

1/2 TEASPOON SALT

1 CUP SOUR CREAM

1/2 POUND FRESH OR FROZEN UNSWEETENED RHUBARB, CUT INTO 1/2-INCH CUBES (ABOUT 1 1/2 CUPS)

SERVES 10 TO 12

1. Preheat the oven to 350 degrees. Grease and flour a 13 by 9 by 2-inch baking pan.

2. In a small bowl, mix together the sugar, nuts, butter, and cinnamon. Using a fork, pastry blender, or your fingers, work this mixture until crumbly. Reserve.

3. In the bowl of an electric mixer set at medium speed and fitted with the paddle attachment, cream together the brown sugar, shortening, and egg for 4 to 5 minutes, or until light and smooth.

4. In a large bowl, whisk together the flour, baking soda, and salt. Whisk eight to nine times to blend. With the mixer on low, add the dry ingredients to the batter, alternating with the sour cream. When smooth, remove from the mixer and stir in the rhubarb.

5. Transfer to the prepared pan and sprinkle evenly with the reserved topping. Bake for 45 to 50 minutes, or until the topping is browned and crisp and the rhubarb squares are cooked through.

6. Serve from the pan, cut into squares.

PAULA'S GINGER-ALMOND COOKIES

I LOVE GINGER. FRESH, PICKLED, CRYSTALLIZED—it's great stuff. Ginger in its various forms is a known remedy for seasickness and these cookies make a great snack for that 10:00 A.M. break on the lobster boat—especially effective on rough days. Dad once employed an island teenager to work in the stern of the *Mattie Belle*. For two consecutive summers, this young man was seasick every single day from the time they left the mooring until they returned several hours later. Paula, the lady friend of an island fisherman, had spent a few days battling seasickness herself and offered my mother this recipe, which she claimed help relieve the symptoms. Mom baked up a batch with the intention of packing a few in Dad's lunch to share with his queasy stern man. The cookies were too good and entirely too much work, Mom decided, to be used medicinally by someone who would not fully enjoy them. She kept the cookies at home and packed Dramamine in the lunchbox instead! *lg*

INGREDIENTS

1 1/2 CUPS (3 STICKS) UNSALTED BUTTER, SOFTENED

1 1/2 CUPS SUGAR

3/4 CUP DARK MOLASSES

4 CUPS ALL-PURPOSE FLOUR

1 1/2 TEASPOONS BAKING SODA

1 1/2 TEASPOONS SALT

1 TABLESPOON PLUS 1 TEASPOON GROUND GINGER

1 TABLESPOON GROUND CINNAMON

1 TABLESPOON GROUND CLOVES

1 1/2 CUPS FINELY CHOPPED ALMONDS

MAKES ABOUT 24 COOKIES

1. In the bowl of an electric mixer fitted with the paddle attachment and set on medium speed, cream the butter, sugar, and molasses for 4 to 5 minutes, or until fluffy.

2. In another bowl, whisk together the flour, baking soda, salt, ginger, cinnamon, and cloves. Whisk eight to ten times.

3. Reduce the speed to low and gradually beat in the dry ingredients. Remove the bowl from the mixer and stir in the almonds.

4. Turn the dough out onto a lightly floured surface. With lightly floured hands, shape the dough into two 2-inch-thick logs. Wrap each log in wax paper and refrigerate for 2 to 3 hours, or overnight, until very firm.

5. Preheat the oven to 350 degrees. Lightly grease a baking sheet.

6. With a serrated knife, slice the logs into 1/4-inch-thick slices. Lay the slices on the baking sheet, leaving about an inch between each one, and bake for 12 to 15 minutes, or until the cookies darken around the edges and are firm. Take care not to overbake.

SIMON'S LEMON TART

THE LAST TIME I MADE THIS TART Linda's boyfriend Simon was a dinner guest. He loved it so much, I decided then and there to name it for him. *mg*

FILLING

2 THIN-SKINNED LEMONS, SEEDED AND THINLY SLICED

5 LARGE EGGS

1 CUP SUGAR

CRUST

1 1/2 CUPS TOASTED CHOPPED WALNUTS (SEE NOTE)

1 1/4 CUPS ALL-PURPOSE FLOUR

1/4 CUP SUGAR

1/2 CUP (1 STICK) UNSALTED BUTTER, SOFTENED AND CUT INTO PIECES

2 TABLESPOONS LIGHTLY BEATEN EGG

TOPPING

1 CUP SUGAR

3/4 CUP ALL-PURPOSE FLOUR

1/2 CUP (1 STICK) UNSALTED BUTTER, CUT INTO SMALL PIECES

LIGHTLY SWEETENED WHIPPED CREAM, FOR SERVING (OPTIONAL)

SERVES 8 TO 10

1. Make the filling. In the bowl of a food processor fitted with the metal blade, pureé the lemon slices. With the motor running, add the eggs, one at a time. Add the sugar and process until well mixed. Transfer to a bowl, cover, and refrigerate for at least 8 hours or overnight.

2. Make the crust. In the bowl of a food processor fitted with the metal blade, pulse the walnuts, flour, and sugar until well mixed and ground. Add the butter and egg and mix until the dough comes together.

3. Press the dough in the bottom and up the sides of a 9-inch tart pan with a removable bottom. Refrigerate for at least 1 hour or overnight.

4. Preheat the oven to 350 degrees.

5. In a small bowl, stir together the sugar and flour. Add the butter and using a fork, pastry blender, or your fingers, work the mixture until it resembles coarse crumbs.

6. Pour the filling into the tart pan, sprinkle evenly with the topping, and bake for 45 to 50 minutes, or until the topping is golden brown and the filling looks set (it will be wobbly in the center).

7. Carefully remove the tart from the pan by removing the bottom of the tart pan. Serve warm, topped with sweetened whipped cream, if desired.

Note

To toast walnuts, spread them on a baking sheet or shallow pan and roast in a 350-degree oven for 8 to 10 minutes, or until lightly browned and fragrant. Let cool, chop, and proceed with the recipe.

The Pie Lady

THE CHALLENGES OF DRIVING ROUTE 1 along coastal Maine in the summer go far beyond bumper-to-bumper traffic and reach deeper than the frustration of being stuck behind two old farts in a Winnebago sporting a bumper sticker that reads I MAY BE SLOW, BUT I'M AHEAD OF YOU! The real trick for me is to successfully avoid all of the foodie landmarks, farm stands, and roadside purveyors of whatever is in season advertised in a barely legible scrawl on a piece of cardboard torn from the box the refrigerator came in. I love to eat and enjoy all types of food, and like hundreds of thousands of other Americans, I am constantly stepping on the scale and wishing that I had not indulged myself.

To transit Route 1 between Portland and Bucksport without giving in to temptation is a true test of willpower and strength of character. I have adapted a slogan from a twelve-step program to help me in my time of need: "One Mile at a Time." I don't usually break out into a cold sweat until I enter the town of Wiscasset, the home of Red's Eats, where touring gourmands devour the tastiest lobster rolls on Mother Earth. Strategically located on the corner of the worst bottleneck and perpetual traffic jam, Red's Eats is impossible to merely ignore and zip on by. My only saving grace is that there is seldom an open parking space.

After Red's, there's a stretch of road that allows me ample time both to *justify* stopping at Moody's Diner and to try to banish the very thought. Lunch at Moody's in Waldoboro would include a mammoth slice of a meat loaf that rivals my mother's. Remembering the diet, I usually manage to cruise right through Waldoboro thinking that I may reward my self-restraint with a pair of hot dogs at Wasses in Belfast.

It takes forever to get to Belfast, but time does nothing to ease the hankering for a couple of those dogs. I'm starving. I have been so good. I haven't eaten a thing all day. I can make decent lobster rolls and adequate meat loaf at home, but Wasses' hot dogs are special. I rarely get by their stand without ordering "two with everything." "Everything" is mustard, relish, and diced onions fried in peanut oil. Oh my God! They are so friggin' good! Now I've blown the diet and know I will make a minimum of two more stops before exiting Route 1. I am weak. I have failed the test and am in a downward spiral.

The next few miles are like running the gauntlet. I am not tempted by "lobsters and seafood packed to travel," for obvious reasons. I may or may not stop at one of the many places that sells homemade ice cream, baked goods, or local corn. I am inclined to yield to blueberries, strawberries, and fresh tomatoes. There's a fifty-fifty chance that I'll board the boat for home with a quiche from the Periwinkle Bakery in Searsport, and more often than not, I will have stopped to see the Pie Lady in Bucksport.

The Pie Lady is the quintessential New England roadside salesman. She has two long tables under a tent in her front yard, and plenty of signs luring passersby to check out the wares. She tactfully displays wooden pie safes with perforated metal doors that allow delicious aromas to seep out and waft around the sales area. Baskets hold beautiful hand-picked produce, and there are mason jars full of yummy-looking canned fruits and veggies. I stop, fully aware that she and her husband who sit and wait under the tent will sell me things that I had no intention of buying. I'll end up with stuff that I neither want nor need. They are nice people. I like them. They engage me in pleasant and interesting conversation while weighing enough tomatoes to feed the island. They seem desperate to get rid of a basket of corn. They ask where I've been and appear to listen intently to my answer as they push jars of jam into the growing pile. I have said "no thanks" to cucumbers twice, but I am certain that I will crumble with the third or fourth plea of "How about a few cukes?" They inquire about my mother and remind me that my father loves lemon meringue pie, of which they just happen to have one left. So, I buy it and am thankful that this is the last penny I will spend as I will soon be free from the hazards of Route 1. The husband helps load my purchases into my car. They smile and wave as I pull out of their driveway. I laugh out loud as I imagine the Pie Lady and her husband folding up their lawn chairs and going home as they have nothing left to sell today. *lg*

MAXINE WRIGHT'S APPLE COBBLER

NOT TOO LONG AGO, Linda rented an apartment in Portland, Maine, for the winter and became friends with her eighty-six-year-old neighbor, Maxine Wright. I met Maxine at a publishing party Linda had at the Dry Dock Bar in Portland, the bar she wrote about in her book *All Fishermen Are Liars*. Maxine and I started swapping stories, and when she learned that Linda and I were working on a cookbook, she offered me her lifetime collection of recipes. I had fun browsing through them and chose this cobbler to include in the book. Thank you, Maxine! *mg*

FILLING

3/4 CUP SUGAR

2 TABLESPOONS ALL-PURPOSE FLOUR

1/2 TEASPOON GROUND CINNAMON

1/4 TEASPOON SALT

2 POUNDS TART, FIRM APPLES, CORED, PEELED, AND THINLY SLICED (ABOUT 5 CUPS)

1 TABLESPOON UNSALTED BUTTER, CUT INTO PIECES

TOPPING

1 CUP SIFTED ALL-PURPOSE FLOUR

1 TABLESPOON SUGAR

1 1/2 TEASPOONS BAKING POWDER

1/2 TEASPOON SALT

3 TABLESPOONS SOLID VEGETABLE SHORTENING OR UNSALTED BUTTER, CUT INTO PIECES

1/2 CUP MILK

SERVES 6

1. Preheat the oven to 400 degrees.

2. Make the filling. In a large bowl, mix together the sugar, flour, cinnamon, and salt. Add the apples and toss to coat with the sugar mixture. Sprinkle 1/4 cup of water over the apples and transfer to a 2 1/2-quart casserole dish.

3. Dot the apples with the butter, cover with foil, and bake for 15 minutes.

4. Meanwhile, make the topping. In a large bowl, whisk together the flour, sugar, baking powder, and salt. Add the shortening or butter and using a fork, pastry blender, or your fingers, work until the mixture resembles coarse crumbs. Add the milk all at once and stir until smooth.

5. Remove the casserole from the oven, remove and discard the foil, and drop the topping batter by spoonfuls on top of the apples to cover.

6. Return to the oven and bake for 25 to 30 minutes longer, or until the topping is lightly browned and firm and the filling is bubbling.

BLONDIES WITH PECANS AND CHOCOLATE CHIPS

THIS IS ONE OF THE RECIPES in the book that I would call old-fashioned only because it's been  around for a long time. My mother used to make these, which are just like brownies without the chocolate in the batter. They are so delicious! *mg*

INGREDIENTS

2 CUPS ALL-PURPOSE FLOUR

1 TEASPOON BAKING POWDER

3/4 TEASPOON SALT

1/4 TEASPOON BAKING SODA

10 TABLESPOONS (1 1/4 STICKS) UNSALTED BUTTER

2 CUPS PACKED LIGHT BROWN SUGAR

2 LARGE EGGS

2 TEASPOONS PURE VANILLA EXTRACT

3/4 CUP CHOPPED PECANS (ABOUT 3 OUNCES)

3/4 CUP SEMISWEET CHOCOLATE CHIPS

SERVES 8 TO 10

1. Preheat the oven to 350 degrees. Butter and flour a 13 by 9 by 2-inch baking pan.

2. In a mixing bowl, whisk together the flour, baking powder, salt, and baking soda. Set aside.

3. In a large saucepan, melt the butter over low heat. Stir in the brown sugar until melted. With the pan off the heat, whisk in the eggs and then the vanilla. Gradually stir in the flour mixture and half of the pecans. The batter will be thick.

4. Spread the batter in the prepared pan and sprinkle evenly with the chocolate chips and the remaining pecans. Bake for about 30 to 35 minutes, or until a toothpick inserted near the center of the blondies comes out with just a few moist crumbs clinging to it.

5. Cool the blondies in the pan on a wire rack. When cool, cut into squares and serve. These may be prepared a day ahead of time, covered, and held at room temperature.

STRAWBERRY SHORTCAKE TRIFLE

THIS IS ONE OF THE PRETTIEST DESSERTS I MAKE. I have a couple of trifle bowls that I really like to use—and I use them every chance I can. When I see strawberries in the market in the summertime, I think of this trifle and if there are a lot of us for dinner, I double or triple it. It's so easy and not too rich, even after a lobster dinner. The island store may not carry much, but it does stock vanilla pudding and frozen pound cake! *mg*

INGREDIENTS

1 PINT FRESH STRAWBERRIES

2 TABLESPOONS SUGAR

2 CUPS HOMEMADE OR PACKAGED INSTANT VANILLA PUDDING

ONE 3-OUNCE PACKAGE CREAM CHEESE, SOFTENED

2 1/2 CUPS 1/2-INCH-THICK CUBES NANA'S POUND CAKE
(PAGE 206) OR STORE-BOUGHT POUND CAKE

LIGHTLY SWEETENED WHIPPED CREAM, FOR GARNISH

SERVES 6 TO 8

1. Reserve 3 or 4 of the best-looking berries for garnish.

2. Hull and slice enough of the remaining berries to measure 2 cups. Set aside.

3. Transfer the remaining berries to the bowl of a food processor fitted with a metal blade, add the sugar, and process to a purée.

4. In the bowl of an electric mixer set on medium speed and fitted with the paddle attachment, beat together the pudding and cream cheese.

5. Arrange the sliced berries around the sides of a clear, straight-sided 1 1/2-quart glass bowl or trifle dish.

6. Spread half of the cake cubes over the bottom of the dish. Pour half of the puréed berries over the cake and top with half of the pudding mixture. Repeat to layer the cake, berries, and pudding mixture.

7. Cover and refrigerate for up to 24 hours. Before serving, top with the whipped cream and reserved strawberries for garnish.

BIBO'S PUMPKIN SQUARES

THESE PUMPKIN SQUARES are a long-standing Thanksgiving tradition at the Greenlaw house, dating back to when my daughter Biffy was ten years old. I fondly remember a day when she accompanied me to the hospital coffee shop where I volunteered with my friend Bibo. Bibo had brought in several batches of these squares to serve at the coffee shop that afternoon, and Biff loved them at first bite. I have been making them ever since at my daughter's request. Biffy even asked for the recipe, which is amazing because to this day she doesn't cook much. *mg*

SQUARES

2 CUPS SUGAR

ONE 15-OUNCE PURE PUMPKIN (ABOUT 2 CUPS)

1 CUP FLAVORLESS VEGETABLE OIL

4 LARGE EGGS

2 CUPS ALL-PURPOSE FLOUR

2 TEASPOONS BAKING POWDER

2 TEASPOONS GROUND CINNAMON

1 TEASPOON BAKING SODA

1/2 TEASPOON SALT

FROSTING

ONE 3-OUNCE PACKAGE CREAM CHEESE, SOFTENED

1 TEASPOON PURE VANILLA EXTRACT

6 TABLESPOONS (3/4 STICK) UNSALTED BUTTER OR MARGARINE, SOFTENED

1 TABLESPOON HEAVY CREAM OR EVAPORATED MILK

1 3/4 CUPS CONFECTIONERS' SUGAR

MAKES 18 TO 24 SQUARES

1. Preheat the oven to 350 degrees. Lightly butter a shallow 10 by 15-inch pan.

2. In the bowl of an electric mixer set on medium speed and fitted with the paddle attachment, beat together the sugar, pumpkin, and oil until smooth. Add the eggs, one at a time, beating well after each addition.

3. In a mixing bowl, whisk together the flour, baking powder, cinnamon, baking soda, and salt. Whisk eight to nine times until well blended.

4. Add the flour mixture to the pumpkin mixture, whisking until well blended. Do not overbeat.

5. Pour into the prepared pan, smooth evenly, and bake for 20 to 25 minutes, or until golden brown and springy and a toothpick inserted in the center comes out clean.

6. Let the pumpkin squares cool in the pan set on a wire rack. When completely cooled, frost.

7. Make the frosting. In the bowl of an electric mixer set on medium speed and fitted with the paddle attachment, beat the cream cheese, vanilla, and butter until smooth. Add the cream and beat until mixed.

8. Gradually add the confectioners' sugar and beat until smooth.

9. Spread the frosting on the cooled pumpkin squares. Cut into squares to serve.

Simple Custard

MY FIRST AND ONLY FORAY INTO INTERNET SHOPPING was during a lapse of common sense when I purchased two tickets to a Neil Diamond concert with which to surprise my boyfriend, Simon, for his birthday. As he is conservative socially and fiscally, he sure was surprised. (I think he was expecting a pair of socks.) "Gee, thanks. I love Neil Diamond. Now all we need are airline tickets to Las Vegas, accommodations, and meals, right?" So, the whole thing ended up being a bit more extravagant than I had planned. Although "wild and crazy" describes neither Simon nor I, we've never been accused of being unadventurous. (Most of our adventures include hiking boots, boats, and peanut butter sandwiches.)

Biff, my younger sister, had been to Las Vegas several times on business and recommended staying at the Bellagio. She told me that *Ocean's Eleven* had been filmed there, and I thought, *If it's good enough for George Clooney, it's good enough for Simon,* and went about the business of securing a room for three nights and making dinner reservations. I had heard and read about the exceptional food at the many marvelous restaurants—even recalled the names of a few of them for the concierge. World-famous celebrity chefs would be cooking for *us*. This was over the top!

By the time we boarded the plane to return to Boston, I had gained enough weight so that my seams were talking. I have eaten in fancy restaurants all over the country, but nothing compared to the abundance and variety on each and every plate set before us in Las Vegas: total gluttony—bordering on the ridiculous. One waiter's enthusiastic recital of the specials had me drop-jawed and in awe of the drama as I vividly and briefly recalled my single competitive oral interpretation of "Casey at the Bat" my sophomore year in high school. That scary memory distracted my ear from the menu just enough so that when I came back to real time my brain was simmering in a cauldron of adjectives, without the slightest hint of a noun.

Appetizers were smoked, creamed, and stuffed. Entrées were infused, braised, spiced, minted, brined, and finished. Desserts were drizzled, candied, and marbled. Three meals a day for three days; even ordering eggs was confusing.

Towering vertical stacks of ingredients from every major food group and beyond were presented by a young man who looked like Liza Minnelli one evening as we sipped the biggest martinis ever made. From our seats we could see both the Eiffel Tower and the Statue of Liberty through fountains that danced to Beethoven. Between courses I had my picture taken with Elvis Presley. Another martini appeared with a platter of food that can best be described as impressionist.

Yes, by the time we boarded that eastbound plane, I refused the bag of pretzels offered by the flight attendant, vowing never to eat again. Birthday socks were gaining potential for next year. I fell into a food- and alcohol-induced coma for the duration of the flight. Dreams of ancho chilies and maraschino cherries performing Cirque du Soleil style faded in and out with the turbulence. Touchdown at Logan was accompanied by a burp from me.

It was nearly midnight when we arrived at Simon's mother's place where we would get a few hours sleep before driving north. I was surprised to see that the nearly one-hundred-year-old woman, Martha Holmes, had waited up for us, shocked that she had cooked something for us, and horrified to think that I might actually have to force something down before bed. "I thought a simple custard would be nice for you to sleep on," she said softly as she set three places at her table.

"Oh, that would be wonderful," was Simon's answer as I rolled my eyes and mouthed, "You're kidding me, right?" But saying "no thanks" to your boyfriend's ninety-nine-year-old mother who has waited until midnight to treat you kindly with something prepared with little more than love was out of the question. I sat. She served. I ate. The tiny cup of plain pale yellow custard disappeared in four bites and was the most delightful thing I had consumed in days. It made me feel good.

"Martha, that was delicious. Thank you."

"It's just a simple custard, but I thought it might taste good to you," she said. How did she know? *lg*

GINGERBREAD WITH CRYSTALLIZED GINGER

HAVE I MENTIONED THAT I LIKE GINGER? It's interesting to note that certain ingredients that become trendy are very often found in a large percentage of old traditional recipes. Crystallized ginger has had its day in the limelight and perhaps will go the way of jicama and other outdated fad foods, but I will always like it in this excellent gingerbread. It's best served warm with a generous dollop of whipped cream. (Although it's passé, I like to add a bit of nutmeg to the whipped cream.) *lg*

INGREDIENTS

1 1/2 CUPS ALL-PURPOSE FLOUR

1 TEASPOON GROUND CINNAMON

3/4 TEASPOON GROUND GINGER

1/2 TEASPOON BAKING SODA

1/2 TEASPOON BAKING POWDER

1/2 TEASPOON SALT

1/4 TEASPOON GROUND NUTMEG

1/2 CUP (1 STICK) UNSALTED BUTTER, AT ROOM TEMPERATURE

1/2 CUP PACKED LIGHT BROWN SUGAR

1/2 CUP DARK MOLASSES

1 LARGE EGG

1/2 CUP HOT WATER

1/4 CUP CHOPPED CRYSTALLIZED GINGER

LIGHTLY SWEETENED WHIPPED CREAM, FOR SERVING

SERVES 8 TO 10

1. Position the oven rack in the center of the oven and preheat the oven to 350 degrees. Butter and flour an 8-inch-square baking pan (a brownie pan).

2. In a mixing bowl, whisk together the flour, cinnamon, ginger, baking soda, baking powder, salt, and nutmeg. Reserve.

3. In the bowl of an electric mixer set on medium speed and fitted with the paddle attachment, beat together the butter and brown sugar for 4 to 5 minutes, or until light and fluffy. Add the molasses, egg, and hot water and beat until blended.

4. With the mixer on low speed, gradually add the dry ingredients until blended. Do not overmix. Stir in the chopped ginger.

5. Spread the batter in the prepared pan and bake for 30 to 35 minutes, or until the top is springy and a toothpick inserted in the center comes out clean.

6. Transfer the pan to a wire rack to cool for about 10 minutes. Run a kitchen knife around the gingerbread and unmold onto the rack to cool completely.

7. Serve warm, topped with whipped cream.

OATMEAL–CHOCOLATE CHIP COOKIES

MY OLDER SISTER AND I have been making these for our children and grandchildren for years and I honestly don't know who gave whom the recipe, but it's a good one. Some family members call these cowboy cookies, although I'm not sure why. I just know they are a great favorite. *mg*

INGREDIENTS

1 CUP SOLID VEGETABLE SHORTENING

1 CUP GRANULATED SUGAR

1 CUP PACKED LIGHT BROWN SUGAR

2 LARGE EGGS

1 TEASPOON PURE VANILLA EXTRACT

2 CUPS ALL-PURPOSE FLOUR

1 TEASPOON BAKING SODA

1/2 TEASPOON SALT

1 CUP OLD-FASHIONED ROLLED OATS

ONE 12-OUNCE PACKAGE CHOCOLATE CHIPS

MAKES 48 TO 60 COOKIES

1. Preheat the oven to 375 degrees. Butter two baking sheets.

2. In the bowl of an electric mixer set on medium speed and fitted with the paddle attachment, cream together the shortening and sugars for 4 to 5 minutes, or until light and fluffy. Add the eggs, one at a time, beating well after each addition. Stir in the vanilla.

3. In a mixing bowl, whisk together the flour, baking soda, and salt. Whisk eight to nine times until well blended. With the mixer on low speed, mix the dry ingredients into the batter just until blended.

4. Remove the bowl from the mixer and stir in the oats and chocolate chips. Drop by teaspoonfuls on the buttered baking sheets, leaving about 1 inch between each cookie. Bake for 9 to 12 minutes, or until lightly browned around the edges.

5. Let the cookies cool on the baking sheets for 3 to 5 minutes and then remove to wire racks to cool.

INDIAN PUDDING

ALTHOUGH I HAVE EATEN IT FOR BREAKFAST, Indian Pudding is one of the more earthy and satisfying desserts to follow a big meal. It's great served warm with a scoop of ice cream. French vanilla or homemade cinnamon ice cream, if you can get it, is fantastic. *lg*

INGREDIENTS

4 CUPS COLD MILK

1/3 CUP YELLOW CORNMEAL

1/2 CUP DARK MOLASSES

1/4 CUP SUGAR

1/4 CUP (1/2 STICK) UNSALTED BUTTER

2 LARGE EGGS, LIGHTLY BEATEN

2 TEASPOONS GROUND GINGER

1 TEASPOON SALT

VANILLA ICE CREAM, FOR SERVING (OPTIONAL)

SERVES 8

1. Preheat the oven to 300 degrees. Lightly butter a 2- to 2 1/2-quart casserole.

2. In a saucepan, heat 2 cups of the milk over medium-high heat until scalding. Do not let it boil, but heat just until small bubbles appear around the edges.

3. Put the cornmeal in the top of a double boiler set over rapidly simmering water and slowly pour the scalded milk into it, stirring until thickened. Cook for about 20 minutes or until thickened.

4. Add the molasses, sugar, butter, eggs, ginger, and salt and mix well. Transfer to the casserole. Add the remaining 2 cups of milk, which should be cold, but do not stir. Bake for about 1 1/2 to 2 hours, or until the pudding is set and lightly browned. The pudding will be a little jiggly in the center.

5. Serve warm with vanilla ice cream, if desired.

THANKSGIVING PUMPKIN PIE WITH WALNUT CRUST

I HAVE NEVER THOUGHT it worthwhile to try to improve too much on the recipe for pumpkin pie on the back of the can of pumpkin. I have dressed it up a little by adding walnuts to the crust, and I choose to use whole milk and cream instead of evaporated milk, but otherwise, it's pretty classic and timeless. We would never dream of Thanksgiving without this pie! *mg*

GRAHAM CRACKER–WALNUT CRUST

9 TO 10 WHOLE GRAHAM CRACKERS (1 WRAPPED PACKET), COARSELY BROKEN

1/2 CUP COARSELY CHOPPED WALNUTS

2 TABLESPOONS PLUS 1 TEASPOON SUGAR

5 TABLESPOONS UNSALTED BUTTER, MELTED

FILLING

ONE 15-OUNCE CAN PURE PUMPKIN (ABOUT 2 CUPS)

3/4 CUP SUGAR

2 LARGE EGGS

1 1/2 TEASPOONS GROUND CINNAMON

1/2 TEASPOON FRESHLY GRATED NUTMEG

1/2 TEASPOON GROUND GINGER

PINCH OF SALT

3/4 CUP MILK

3/4 CUP HEAVY CREAM

SERVES 8 TO 10

1. Preheat the oven to 350 degrees.

2. In the bowl of a food processor fitted with the metal blade, process the graham crackers and walnuts to fine crumbs. Add the sugar and pulse to mix. With the motor running, add the butter until absorbed.

3. Press the graham cracker mixture over the bottom and up the sides of a 9-inch pie plate. Bake for 10 to 12 minutes, or until nearly set. The crust will firm up as it cools. Cool completely on a wire rack. Do not turn off the oven but increase the temperature to 375 degrees.

4. In a mixing bowl, stir together the pumpkin and sugar with a wooden spoon. Add the eggs and beat well. Add the cinnamon, nutmeg, ginger, and salt and mix well. Gently whisk in the milk and cream until smooth.

5. Pour the filling into the cooled pie shell. Smooth the top and bake for 40 to 45 minutes, or until the filling is set but still a little wobbly in the center.

6. Let the pie cool on a wire rack before serving.

MIDNIGHT CUPCAKES OR SNACK CAKE WITH CREAM CHEESE FROSTING

I DON'T BAKE A LOT OF CAKES but this easy chocolate one is a family favorite. I make it plain, without frosting, as a snack cake to have in the house for the grandchildren, and it makes very good cupcakes with fluffy white frosting. *mg*

CAKE

1 CUP HOT WATER

1/2 CUP UNSWEETENED COCOA POWDER

1 1/4 CUPS GRANULATED SUGAR

1/2 CUP SOLID VEGETABLE SHORTENING OR UNSALTED BUTTER

2 LARGE EGGS

1 1/2 CUPS ALL-PURPOSE FLOUR

1 TEASPOON BAKING SODA

1 TEASPOON BAKING POWDER

1/2 TEASPOON SALT

1 TEASPOON PURE VANILLA EXTRACT

CREAM CHEESE FROSTING

3/4 CUP (1 1/2 STICKS) UNSALTED BUTTER, AT ROOM TEMPERATURE

ONE 8-OUNCE PACKAGE CREAM CHEESE

1 TO 1 1/4 CUPS CONFECTIONERS' SUGAR

1 TABLESPOON MILK

1/2 TEASPOON PURE VANILLA EXTRACT

MAKES 14 TO 16 CUPCAKES OR 1 SNACK CAKE

1. Preheat the oven to 350 degrees. Lightly butter two 8-cup muffin tins or insert paper liners into the cups. If making a snack cake, lightly butter an 8-inch-square pan (a brownie pan) and line it with wax paper.

2. In a mixing bowl, whisk the water into the cocoa slowly. When smooth, set aside.

3. In the bowl of an electric mixer fitted with the paddle attachment and set on medium speed, cream the sugar and shortening for 4 to 5 minutes, or until light and fluffy. Add the eggs, one at a time, beating well after each addition.

4. In a mixing bowl, whisk together the flour, baking soda, baking powder, and salt. Whisk 8 to 9 times until well blended.

5. Add the dry ingredients to the wet ingredients, alternating with the cocoa, beating at medium speed until well mixed. Beat in the vanilla.

6. Spoon the batter into the cupcake cups, filling each about two-thirds full, or pour into the square pan. Bake the cupcakes for 18 to 20 minutes and the snack cake for 50 to 55 minutes. When done, a toothpick inserted in the center of a cupcake or the snack cake will come out clean.

7. Let the cupcakes or snack cake cool in the pan set on a wire rack.

8. Meanwhile, make the frosting. In the bowl of an electric mixer set on medium speed and fitted with the paddle attachment, beat the butter and cream cheese until smooth. Add the sugar, alternating with the milk, and beat until creamy. Stir in the vanilla.

9. When cool, frost with the cream cheese frosting.

ISLAND APPLE PIE

THIS PIE FILLING IS ALL MY OWN CREATION. My mother baked magnificent pies and was well known for them. When I was growing up, we each got to pick the kind of pie she would make that week for Sunday dinner and I usually chose apple. My brother Freeman chose lemon meringue, Chuckie chose blueberry, Gracie chose pecan, Avis asked for graham cracker pie, and Gary just loved them all! When I decided to make my own apple pie, I made the filling with lots of citrus for its fresh, clean taste. The crust uses only vegetable shortening because that's how my mother made it. If I see a pie crust recipe that calls for butter, I'll try it. *mg*

FLAKY PIE CRUST

2 1/4 CUPS COLD ALL-PURPOSE FLOUR

3/4 CUP COLD SOLID VEGETABLE SHORTENING

1 TEASPOON SALT

5 TO 6 TABLESPOONS ICE WATER

FILLING

4 POUNDS GRANNY SMITH OR OTHER FIRM, TART APPLES

3/4 CUP SUGAR, PLUS 1 TEASPOON FOR SPRINKLING

1 TABLESPOON FRESH LEMON JUICE

1 TEASPOON FRESH ORANGE JUICE

ZEST OF 1 LEMON OR 1 SMALL ORANGE

1/4 CUP ALL-PURPOSE FLOUR

3/4 TEASPOON GROUND CINNAMON

1/2 TEASPOON FRESHLY GRATED NUTMEG

SERVES 8 TO 10

1. Make the crust. In a mixing bowl, whisk the flour several times to aerate it. Add half of the shortening to the bowl and using two knives, a fork, pastry blender, or your fingers, work the shortening into the flour until it resembles coarse meal. Add the remaining shortening and work it in until it resembles small peas.

2. Dissolve the salt in 5 tablespoons of the water and add to the flour mixture. Stir lightly with a fork. If the mixture holds together, do not add the remaining tablespoon of water. If it's too dry, add the rest of the water.

3. Gently gather the dough into a mass and wrap it in wax paper. Refrigerate for at least 30 minutes or as long as overnight.

4. Preheat the oven to 350 degrees.

5. Remove the dough from the refrigerator and let it sit at room temperature for about 10 minutes to get the chill off. Divide the dough into two pieces, one slightly larger than the other. Return the smaller piece to the refrigerator.

6. On a lightly floured surface, roll the larger piece of dough into a circle about 12 inches in diameter. Carefully drape the dough in a 9-inch pie dish, pressing gently along the bottom and up the sides. Leave the overhang.

7. Peel, core, and slice the apples into thin wedges or small chunks.

8. In a large bowl, toss the apples with the sugar, juices, and zest. Add the flour, cinnamon, and nutmeg and toss to coat. Spoon the apple mixture into the pie crust.

9. Remove the other piece of dough from the refrigerator and let it sit for about 10 minutes before rolling on a lightly floured surface to a diameter of 11 inches. Drape over the top of the pie. Turn the bottom overhang up over the top crust, trim any excess, and using a fork, crimp the two crusts together. Vent the top crust with two or three small slits.

10. Bake in the center of the oven for about 1 hour, or until the crust is lightly browned and the filling is bubbling. If the edge of the crust gets a little dark, shield with aluminum foil.

11. Let the pie cool on a wire rack before serving.

Acknowledgments

———

FOREMOST, I WOULD LIKE TO THANK MY MOTHER for the amazing amount of work she has done on this project. What a monumental task it had to be for her to go through fifty years of accumulated notes and recipe cards. She actually learned to use the computer at age seventy, which reminds me to thank my dad profusely for teaching her. That truly could not have been much fun as Mom tends to be a bit dramatic.

Thanks as ever to my literary agent, Stuart Krichevsky. Many thanks to all of the great folks at Hyperion, especially Will Schwalbe. Will, my editor and friend, is solely responsible for the unique opportunity for me to work with my mother. And thanks to Emily Gould for her creative suggestions and her help in putting all the pieces together. I know how lucky we are to have a publicist like Christine Ragasa, a marketing genius like Jane Comins, and Phil Rose in the art department. Working with two Greenlaw women must surely have tested patience.

And we also want to thank Sara Gray, for her beautiful pictures of our beloved "very small" island, and of us, and for her stunning photographs of other parts of Maine. And thanks to Joseph DeLeo, for his wonderful food photography, and to food stylist Suzette Kaminsky and prop stylist Gigi Scandinaro. And thanks to Fish's Eddy for letting them borrow so much stuff. Thanks also to Timothy Hsu for his design talents.

Although Mom was initially insulted by the notion of recipe testers—after all, "these recipes have been tested for fifty years"—in the end, we both owe much thanks to Mary Goodbody and Brooke Dojny for all they have done in putting this book together, which goes far beyond the testing of recipes. They are amazing!

Finally, Mom wishes to express special thanks and appreciation to her gourmet group, bridge gals, island friends, and Ginny Brehmer. *Linda*

ILLUSTRATION INDEX

ALMOND

APPLE

BEAN

BEEF

BEET

BLUEBERRIES

CARROT

CHERRIES

CHICKEN

CLAM

CLOVE

COD

CORN

CRAB

CRANBERRIES

EGG

FLOUR

GREEN BEAN

HADDOCK

HAKE

HALIBUT

HEN

HORSE MACKEREL

LAMB

LEMON

LETTUCE

LOBSTER

MUSHROOM

MUSSEL

NUTS

OAT

ONION

OYSTER

PEA BEANS

PECAN

PORK

POTATO

PUMPKIN

RICE

SALMON

SCALLOP

SOLE

SPINACH

STRAWBERRY

SWEET POTATO

SWORDFISH

TOMATO

TUNA

TURKEY

VENISON

WALNUT

WHEAT

• RECIPES FROM A VERY SMALL ISLAND •

INDEX

NOTES

NOTES